I0762711

# ENDORSEMENTS

I've watched Steve Kang live every day; he has an unquenchable passion to reach one more soul because he really knows firsthand the kindness and severity of the Lord! Steve does not have an "off" button because the love of Christ compels him to champion soul-winning. I highly recommend this timely and terrifying book; but even more so, I recommend the yielded and compassionate vessel through whom the Lord has released this book. May your heart be stirred with Heaven's cry.

**Daniel Park**
Lead Pastor, Jesus Center

Steve Kang's gripping near-death experience gives powerful evidence for the reality of hell, Heaven, and the loving God of mercy who rescued Steve when he took his own life after a 10-day drug binge. Nothing else explains this young Buddhist's transformation from a drug addict to a Christian pastor except the reality of the God Steve now passionately serves. Steve's story will keep you turning pages and leave you in awe of God's lovingkindness and grace offered to every person.

**John Burke, Pastor**
Author of *The New York Times* bestseller *Imagine Heaven* and *Imagine the God of Heaven*

As his mentor, the Pastor Steve Kang I know is a revivalist who only preaches Jesus Christ and the Kingdom of God. He is a man of God who dreams of even one soul returning to the Lord through the grace of the Gospel of Jesus Christ in the last days. This book will help you catch that desire.

**Joseph Lee, Pastor**
Founder, Loving Jesus Ministry

I have been in full-time ministry since 1996 and have never heard a testimony like the one from my friend Steve Kang. *8 Hours in Hell* will awaken your heart to the reality of eternity and how we must get to work obeying the Great Commission. Steve is truly a genuine, humble soul who walks in the supernatural power of the Holy Spirit. Get ready for your life to be set on fire as you read this book.

**Erwin Guevara, Senior Pastor**
New Dawn LA
Founding Apostle, Jesus Movement Network

Steve Kang is a powerful man of God who has encountered the Lord in a profound way and serves with passionate devotion. His unwavering testimony and deep love for Jesus inspire many to follow the Savior.

**Sinwoong Park, Senior Pastor**
Irvine Onnuri (All Nations) Church

Pastor Steve Kang is one of the most passionate individuals I've ever met when it comes to evangelism and loving God. His testimony about Heaven and hell has the power to awaken souls and has led countless individuals to Christ. He is a man of genuine faith, living wholeheartedly before God. I sincerely hope this book will become a precious channel for spreading the Gospel.

**Pastor Scott Park, Senior Pastor**
Toronto Cross Church, Canada

As a friend of Steve Kang for the past two decades, his story is a testimony of what Christ can do to save a lost soul and use that very person to save others. Steve's passion and love for Jesus are so genuine and inspirational, and this devotion has never waned in all my years of knowing him. You will be touched by his testimony and stirred to follow Christ wholeheartedly.

**Joon Lee**
Grace Ministries International
Pastor and Director of Education

*8 Hours in Hell* is a gripping, life-changing testimony that will shake you to your core. Steve shares his harrowing journey of dying, experiencing the torment of hell, and being given a second chance to encounter the glory of Heaven. His story of radical transformation and newfound passion for Jesus is a vivid reminder of God's relentless love and mercy. This is more than a book—it's an invitation to encounter the truth that changes everything. Steve is one of the most passionate followers of Jesus I have met, and his testimony is saving lives. We are saved by the blood of the Lamb and the Word of our testimony! (Revelation 12:11)

**Julie Hedenborg**
Creator and Host of *Everyday Miracles Podcast*
Christian Author and Speaker

Loved and honored across generations—especially by the young—this humble, passionate man of God carries a message with eternal weight. What he shares in these pages is nothing less than life-altering truth for our time.

**Jason Kim, Next Gen Pastor**
New Song Evangelical Church

Steve Kang's *8 Hours in Hell* is a powerful testimony that inspires and challenges the body of Christ. His extraordinary encounter is not only gripping but also a profound reminder of God's grace, deliverance, and the reality of spiritual warfare. I'm honored to have walked and witnessed how God has used and continues to use Pastor Steve all these years. This book is a timely encouragement for believers seeking to deepen their faith and walk boldly in God's truth.

**Jack Lee, Senior Pastor**
Impact Harvest Church, California

Raw, riveting, and impossible to ignore. *8 Hours in Hell* is a gripping account of one man's terrifying descent into darkness and the redemptive power of Jesus Christ. This testimony is more than just a wake-up call, it's a blazing reminder of eternity's reality and the transforming grace of God. If you've ever questioned the afterlife—or the urgency of salvation—this book demands your attention.

**Captain Dale Black**
Bestselling Author of *Atomic Faith*; *Life, Cancer and God*; *Flight to Heaven*; and *Visiting Heaven*

# 8 HOURS *in* HELL

A SHOCKING FIRSTHAND EXPERIENCE
OF WHAT REALLY AWAITS
IN THE AFTERLIFE

Steve Kang

© Copyright 2025– Steve Kang

All rights reserved. This book is protected by the copyright laws of the United States of America. This book may not be copied or reprinted for commercial gain or profit. The use of short quotations or occasional page copying for personal or group study is permitted and encouraged. Permission will be granted upon request. Scripture quotations marked NKJV are taken from the New King James Version. Copyright © 1982 by Thomas Nelson, Inc. Used by permission. All rights reserved. Scripture quotations marked ESV are taken from The Holy Bible, English Standard Version® (ESV®), copyright © 2001 by Crossway, a publishing ministry of Good News Publishers. Used by permission. All rights reserved. Scripture quotations marked NIV are taken from the HOLY BIBLE, NEW INTERNATIONAL VERSION®, Copyright © 1973, 1978, 1984, 2011 International Bible Society. Used by permission of Zondervan. All rights reserved. Scripture quotations marked KJV are taken from the King James Version. All emphasis within Scripture quotations is the author's own. Take note that the name satan and related names are not capitalized. We choose not to acknowledge him, even to the point of violating grammatical rules.

DESTINY IMAGE® PUBLISHERS, INC.
P.O. Box 310, Shippensburg, PA 17257-0310
*"Publishing cutting-edge prophetic resources to supernaturally empower the body of Christ"*

This book and all other Destiny Image and Destiny Image Fiction books are available at Christian bookstores and distributors worldwide.

For more information on foreign distributors, call 717-532-3040.
Reach us on the Internet: www.destinyimage.com.

ISBN 13 TP: 979-8-8815-0376-5
ISBN 13 eBook: 979-8-8815-0377-2
Hardcover: 979-8-8815-0379-6
Large Print: 979-8-8815-0380-2

For Worldwide Distribution, Printed in the U.S.A.
1 2 3 4 5 6 7 8 / 29 28 27 26 25

# CONTENTS

# FOREWORD

Years ago, I interviewed Steve Kang about his hellacious experience for my *Revelations From* Heaven podcast and for my *Heaven Encounters* broadcast on Sid Roth's ISN network. My first impression was that the person I was interviewing as a pastor was not the same person he was describing to me during his *8 Hours in Hell.* His before (Christ) and after (Christ) personas were diametrically different. I can think of no story that better demonstrates the transformative power of God's Holy Spirit than Steve's. If ever there was a testimony of being born again into a new creation (2 Corinthians 5:17), it is this one.

I have now publicly shown hundreds of near-death and afterlife stories, and my team and I have interviewed over one thousand people who claim to have been to Heaven or hell. Steve's story is distinguished because he bears out in real life what Jesus stated in Matthew 7:16-20, *"You shall know them by their fruits" (verse 16 KJV).* In those verses, Jesus describes how once one becomes a "new creation" (2 Corinthians 5:17), he (or she) bears the fruit of their new existence. Later, in Galatians 5:22-23 those fruits are described: love, joy, peace, patience, kindness, goodness, faithfulness, gentleness, and self-control.

Steve has demonstrated each one of those fruits through our many interactions. But the "old Steve" was the proverbial guy you would never want your daughter to date. In his before-Christ (BC) life, he claimed to be a Buddhist who was no more enlightened than your average drug addict. His partying led to the most severe form of self-injury. He had no peace, to put it mildly, and demonstrated the antithesis of the "fruits of the Spirit."

So, what changed him? Obviously, the one true God (of the Bible). But he also benefited from the power of a praying mother and the intercession of his mother's church members. Steve's story in *8 Hours in Hell* is the embodiment of the Christian faith. No other religion transforms someone so completely and evidentially as does Christianity. Steve is a living testimony of the power of Jesus Christ to completely transform a life.

Like Steve, I died and experienced the afterlife, but unlike Steve, I went to Heaven as a Christian. I think Steve's story is unique because he believed in a religion (Buddhism) in search of enlightenment, but instead, he tried to kill himself after being met by a demonic figure. Who better to describe the power of being reborn (through Christ) than someone who previously believed in a cycle of rebirth?

As you read this book, think of the person who wrote it. Perhaps I could better say, think of the One who was behind the one who wrote this book. You will find the Holy Spirit within the author's expressions. His words will speak in these pages. His love will touch you through the sentiments conveyed. Find the Author of Love through the expression of a man (Steve Kang) who survived hell because of the grace of God.

There is no greater testimony than a man destined for hell, saved by grace, through the power of prayer. Pray for the lost, that they might be saved as was Steve and so many of us who did not deserve the true gift of Christ's salvation but found it because He first loved us (1 John 4:19). Know the transformative power of God by your confession of Jesus as Lord, through a belief in your heart that God raised Him from the dead (Romans 10:9-10). Do as Steve Kang did and live bountifully, as does this beloved pastor today. Thank you, Steve, for blessing us with your story and life.

Randy Kay
CEO, Randy Kay Ministries
Pastor, My Family
Host, *Revelations From Heaven* and *Heaven Encounters*
Author, *Heaven Stormed* and *Revelations From Heaven*

# FOREWORD

I first heard about Pastor Steve Kang through a documentary on near-death experiences, but it wasn't until I met him in person that I truly grasped the weight of his testimony. Since then, I have had the privilege of meeting him numerous times and even hosting him at our church. He is a man who genuinely loves Jesus, walks in the fear of God, and carries a deep passion for evangelism. Of all the testimonies I have encountered, his is one of the most powerful I have ever heard—and the fruit of his ministry confirms its validity.

The reality of eternity is not something we can afford to ignore. Every person will exist forever—whether in Heaven or in hell. You do not decide if you will live forever; you only decide where you will live forever. Jesus Himself spoke more about hell than anyone else in Scripture. Hell is not just for the "super bad," as if it were some kind of maximum-security prison—it is the default destination of humanity apart from salvation in Christ. Hell has no exits. Once there, there is no escape.

Yet, today, Jesus offers hope and salvation. His sacrifice on the Cross provides the only way out of eternal separation from God. This book does more than just recount a terrifying experience—it brings the truth of eternity to the forefront and ignites a fresh passion and conviction to win the lost. May *8 Hours in Hell* awaken your heart, stir your spirit, and embolden you to share the Gospel like never before.

Vladimir Savchuk
Pastor, HungryGen
Author, *Host the Holy Ghost*

# PREFACE

This book reveals my testimony—from Buddhism to Christianity through Jesus and a near-death experience. It is my journey from skepticism of Christianity to profound belief and trust in Jesus. The moment of spiritual realization about the existence of hell led to a personal, life-altering awakening!

Whether young or old, whatever nationality, rich or poor, sick or healthy, male or female, a human is born having questions and seeking answers to the purpose of life. Everyone worships something or someone and seeks fulfillment and true peace in life.

Growing up in a Buddhist home, I was very dedicated and sought to reach Nirvana from the young age of 5. I followed my grandmother, and later my aunt, to the Buddhist temples and spent many hours there in meditation and prayer. I had questions such as: "What is the purpose of life? Is there life after death? What is really good and evil, and the source or reason for injustice?" These questions always caught my heart and attention ever since childhood.

I was taught about spirituality by the monks and my grandmother, and therefore I thought Buddhism was the answer as a young South Korean child. I often thought Christianity was just a made-up story to destroy Eastern nationalism. Some of my Christian friends were hypocrites and this only reinforced the erroneous assumption; though they invited me to church at times.

However, I met Jesus Christ, the only way to the Father and only Savior of the world, through a near-death accident (NDE) and an out-of-body experience (OBE). I met Him after seeing Heaven and hell in the spiritual world.

The purpose and motive for writing this book is to reach one more for Jesus, and to revive one more person in the church if possible, by the grace of God; for one soul is more precious than all of the created universe weighed and put together on a scale. The ultimate purpose of faith is to go to Heaven, and for an unbeliever and skeptic to become a believer.

This book is about my 8-hour journey in hell and what I learned about the eternal state of the soul, after death. After seeing hell and Heaven and encountering Jesus Christ, my life and heart, my inner world, changed drastically—and the Bible showed me that what I experienced was already written in God's Book, the Bible, the Word of God.

# 1

# MY CHILDHOOD STORY

## A CHILD'S QUESTIONS REGARDING LIFE

I was born in Seoul in 1979 and raised in South Korea until I was 9 years old. I have fond memories of sleeping in a cozy room with my grandfather, grandmother, aunts, and a family of 10 or so. My grandfather was a rice wine company president, and I was proud to have him as my grandfather for he was influential in our small city in the south of South Korea—and always gave me small allowances to buy snacks. In his house, my aunts and uncle were there living with me, and we always had thankful family meals, though the choice of food was often limited.

However, my parents were far from me and could not stay in the same house because they were preparing for our immigration to a place called the United States. Until I was 5 years old, my younger brother and I lived with our parents. My father was a very successful businessman owning many furniture stores and seafood companies, but then went bankrupt. My mother, as a result, immigrated to the United States when I was 8 years old in order to transfer her Registered Nurse license to America, to prepare a better future for my brother and me.

Unfortunately, no one in our family went to church at the time. Though I attended a Christian kindergarten, I never heard the Gospel there or attended worship service. My brother, John, who is two years younger, always moved along with me during our frequent relocations.

I started following my grandmother and an aunt to the temples from the age of 6, and I fell in love with Buddhism. I was different from other children who went in and out casually. I was devoted and even slept at the temple. As the time I spent there increased, more questions like the ones mentioned in the Preface began to arise: "Why are humans born? What is the purpose of mankind? What is the meaning of life? Why is there evil and suffering in the world? Why are some born poor, others rich? How do I gain eternal life? What happens after we die?"

At the time, I had no idea what Christianity was, nor had I ever read the Bible. Buddhism was the only religion before me to guide and answer my spiritual curiosities. I remember often seeing evil spirits in my dreams, and I thought it was a normal occurrence for all children.

## LIFE IN BOSTON, USA

I immigrated to America when I was 9 years old. At that time in Boston, Massachusetts, in the late 1980s, I was shocked to see gigantic supermarkets, toy stores, McDonalds, and large restaurants that were not even imaginable in South Korea. I was in awe at first sight. Everything was so pleasant in the United States of America, and I especially loved the generous Thanksgiving tables with so much food and the toys I received on Christmas Day. Newly made friends at Northeast elementary school were all kind to me, the new immigrant student from Asia in the classroom.

### SCHOOL DAYS

Thereafter I entered middle school and was faced with an identity crisis. Some people call it adolescence, but mine was perhaps a bit more extreme than others. I often asked my mom, "Why am I Korean and different from the other ethnicities here?" At that time, in the late '80s and early '90s, there were not many Asians in Boston, especially in the countryside town of Bedford where I lived. White people, black people, and Puerto Ricans were predominant; and Koreans like me were a very small minority.

Being different caused chaos within me as an adolescent, and that chaos turned into anger, and that anger erupted into moody rebellions. I listened to heavy metal music, alternative music, then rap music, all to seek some solace and a sense of identity. None of that provided any healing to my heart. Eventually, a severe depression overshadowed me. Anger can cause depression and lethargy, which I soon found out for myself. And not having Jesus Christ, God, at the time, obviously did not help either.

After my father heard about my rebelliousness in school and disrespect for my mother, he had us move back to South Korea in the fall of 1994. I had spent a total of six years in the Boston area, and just when I made some friends, and even liked a girl classmate, I had to move again. I had always thought I would live in Boston for a long time, so moving all of a sudden was a surprise. I was so turbulent and empty inside at the time, and I just could not understand why I felt that way. I did not know where I really fit in, nor did I have any life goals as a freshman in high school.

I know many high school freshmen do not have goals, but my classmates seemed to be more focused and they fit in better than I did, or I thought at least. I could not focus or study, and though I played some sports, growing up there without my dad present and my mother working a lot did not help me discover or grow my identity. I prayed to Buddha on my own, since no temples were around, and that did not help at all. So reluctantly, I agreed to move back to Seoul, South Korea, in order to attend Seoul International School, a prestigious international school at the time.

## BACK IN SOUTH KOREA

Life and society were very different in South Korea in 1994 than in Boston. First of all, there were so many people everywhere compared to Boston, a town of 10,000 total population. Second, everyone spoke Korean, and my Korean peers respected and even idolized those of us who attended Seoul International School, for speaking English and coming from more prestigious families. I thought I had my identity strengthened more than before. My grades even improved from when I was in Boston. With my dad around in person and with my Korean-American peers all studying, I too decided to study a bit more.

I took AP (advanced placement) classes, earned my Taekwondo 2$^{nd}$ degree black belt, had a college girlfriend who lived nearby, and went to the temple weekly. I woke up daily at 5:30 a.m. just to meditate, chant, and apply what the Buddhist monks taught me spiritually. I even wrote on a poster the 36 laws, or commandments, not 10, that they emphasized, and I taped them to my bedroom wall.

However, I was very disappointed with my moral shortcomings every day I returned home from school. Every day I broke one or more laws. I would reflect upon my day's happenings and my internal state, and every day something was off. Peace came for a few minutes here and there as a Buddhist but soon evaporated. I simply could not grasp peace or make it last.

Reading the 36 moral laws on the wall was a daily habit for me, on top of meditating. On the weekends, I would go to the temple, even bringing my high school peers who were not religious, to meditate all day long. I prayed 8 hours some Saturdays and Sundays, and I strived to reach nirvana. Why? The monks taught me that there is no beginning or end for our life cycles, which by the way is logically impossible since we cannot reach a finite point in history, today for example, by traversing infinity. I will explain more on this topic later in the book.

The monks also explained that it was my previous life's sins that made me who I am today. In order to have a more rich, famous, blessed life in my next life, I need to eradicate my past life's sins by praying in the temple and doing good deeds. I asked them a fair question at that point, "How long will it take for me to erase all my previous lives' sins?" They answered, "Millions of years." Thereafter, one can reach nirvana, or an eternal blissful state of isolation and self-reliance where you are then alone forever, like a god. That is the concept of eternal life in Buddhism they taught me. To reach those two goals. I prayed daily and tried not to sin, so I can have a better next life; and one day, to eventually reach nirvana.

With this intense spiritual discipline, I graduated high school in 1997 and was admitted to a prestigious liberal arts college in Southern California. I moved to Claremont, California, and have been living in Southern California ever since. I studied hard and partied hard, a motto there for some students.

There were Christians at the school, but they never shared the Gospel with me, with the exception of one classmate named Mary. She was a pastor's daughter and would often pray for me and invite me to picnics on the school lawns to eat with her parents. Other than Mary, not one person shared the Gospel with me. As a Buddhist and without the grace of God, I could not understand the truths of the Gospel, Jesus Christ, or the Bible. In preparation to become an attorney in the future, I studied diligently and hoped for the best. Then the summer of 1998 arrived.

My father, a wealthy and successful businessman, called me on a sunny warm, typical day in May 1998. He explained that Korea went through a financial crises, the entire nation, and that all his businesses had to abruptly shut down. At first, I thought he was being humorous. But then I realized he was serious while he was explaining to me how I had to find a place to live, apply for next year's scholarship, and get a job to make money for food, I knew life would be changing dramatically, again. Little did I expect that this would be the beginning of the God of the Bible drawing me closer to Him and to His Son, Jesus Christ.

## TROUBLE BREWING

I did not know about drugs at the time. I hated even the smell of cigarettes. However, based on my testimony you are about to read, you might presume that I did recreational and illegal drugs for a long time, but I had not. I first started smoking marijuana occasionally with friends when I was a freshman in college. The one house that I found to live in during the summer of 1998 was actually a house for frequent drug deals. The guy was a friend of mine from high school, but I did not realize until I moved in how heavily he was involved in drugs. Before long, we were also involved in the transport and trade of cannabis in quantities that could fill our backpacks, and the smoking of cannabis increased to several times a day, without missing a single day. Soon, I started smoking marijuana more than three times a day, every day.

During that entire summer, I do not remember being sober for a more than an hour here and there. We partied and got into trouble. The group of us who met there had the same haircuts, and we met to have fun and get high. I saw people who were addicted to all sorts of drugs and from all states of life, whether poor or rich, who were enslaved by drug addiction. I did not admit it at the time, but upon reflection, I was one of them as well.

When the fall 1998 semester started, I was so addicted and affected by drug use that I did not even have the mental strength to go to class. An acquaintance I met at a party smoked with me again during the first week of that fall semester, saying it was marijuana. However, it was not just marijuana. It was actually laced with some of the worst drugs among all the drugs (heroin, cocaine, PCP, etc.) that people on the streets called "deathbowl."

## 2

# MEETING JESUS CHRIST DURING A NEAR-DEATH EXPERIENCE

When I smoked deathbowl, I stayed up for 10 consecutive nights without any sleep. On the third or fourth day, I began to forget everything, even who I was. I lost the sense of date and time. Around days 8 and 9, my sense of hopelessness, depression, fear, panic, and anxiety reached a zenith. Now I know that it was satan causing such feelings, but at the time, I did not even know who satan was. And without being aware of it, I encountered him with my eyes wide open. He looked just like an ordinary Asian grandfather, and he tried to comfort me saying that he knew how hard my suffering was, and I agreed as he spoke to me.

At the time I did not personally know Jesus Christ and was spiritually blind, thinking this grandfather figure was just another Buddhist god. He appeared to me and said, "Sacrifice your life to me," and that if I would cut my neck and stomach open to end my life, he would save me from hell—50,000 less years of hell to be exact. I did the math, and concluded that a few minutes of earthly pain is worth exchanging for 50,000 less years of hell.

I remember writing a letter to my mom, specifically apologizing to her for failing her in this life, and that I would go ahead of her into the netherworld and reunite with her there. It was the most depressing, fearful, confusing, and hopeless day of my life and my family's. I called the monks for spiritual guidance, but they all single-heartedly answered that they were in the midst of a silent prayer and could not talk to me. I was so disappointed at their selfishness. Without God in my life, I had no power at all over the situation and the devil devoured me, or so I thought.

So I did what the Buddhist spirit asked of me. It was day 10 of staying awake, and I was at home with my mom who was in the house somewhere. I went to the kitchen, opened the drawers to look for the biggest knife I could find, and got on my knees. I even had my Jansport bag on my back with my wallet and the Buddhist prayer book in it, in case I might be able to take them to the afterlife.

Holding the knife, I wasn't sure where or how to begin. So I started cutting my throat and then split open my stomach, bleeding so much that I ended up losing the majority of my blood. When my mom saw me with the knife and bleeding in the living room, she immediately called 911.

The police and other ambulance staff arrived within minutes. This all happened in the city of Irvine, where the police are quickly responsive. Because of my violently agitated and dangerous behavior, the police officers subdued me as I struggled against them, pepper sprayed me, and even had to hit me several times with their batons. The pain was so excruciating that I dropped the knife and collapsed. The majority of the living room carpet was covered in blood, as the apartment managers and my mom recall.

When I arrived at the UC Irvine Medical Center, I was fading in and out of consciousness. While in the ambulance and before entering the surgery room, I could feel my soul leaving my body, and I began to have what is called an out-of-body experience (OBE). I actually saw myself on the stretcher and then lying on the operating table, unconscious and laying still. It was the weirdest feeling and sight, to see my own self but to not be in my own body.

Soon thereafter, I started to fall into an endless abyss, with the same feeling as if I was falling in an elevator or going down a hill on a rollercoaster. I expected to go up to Heaven, but the exact opposite happened. After about 5 minutes, I landed in what I now know is hell, according to the Bible. I was suddenly struck with tremendous fear, the fear that I was now completely abandoned, a fear one hundred times more painful than any pain I had ever felt in my earthly life. How did I know I was actually in hell? It was a sight I had never thought of or ever imagined before—and there were countless people there.

## IN HELL

Demons wearing capes were everywhere, big ones as tall as a few stories and even taller—not the small ones you see in cartoons. I tangibly felt the pain of hell there, and I became conscious of the fact that I was a sinner for the very first time. On earth, though I was not perfect, I was a considerably good person, in my opinion. I never killed anyone or sold really harmful drugs. I lied and cheated, but that was for the "greater good." Now, I knew I deserved hell, and it was the most painful feeling ever in my heart. The physical, spiritual, mental, and emotional pain there in hell is something I pray nobody feels, not even my worst enemies. Also, I supernaturally knew that I would be trapped there forever and ever.

Only then I realized how wrong the grandfather figure was when he promised to take me to nirvana, and what a grave mistake I had made. The devil came into my life to steal, kill, and destroy me (John 10:10) and he deceived me by masquerading as an angel of light (2 Corinthians 11:14). In the United States alone, an average of 48 people commit suicide daily, or one every 30 minutes. Because of what I did to myself, I was about to become a statistic, forgotten in eternal hell by God Himself and all of humanity and history, forever.

On earth, God shines His sunlight and sends rain even on the wicked (Matthew 5:45). It is called "common grace" in Christian theology. However, in hell, there is not an iota of God or His mercy or light. It was total darkness—there were no plants, no animals, no kids;

just people screaming in agony. The pain was so excruciating for me that I could not ask any questions of the others. The ground was so barren, rocky cliffs to my right and left, the sky or space above me total darkness.

As a sinner who deserved hell forever, I experienced eternal separation from God. And yet I was allowed to return to earth to share about its reality. If one less human being, soul, does not go to hell as a result of my sharing, all the pain and agony was worth it! By His mercy and perfect planning and purposes, which I do not fully comprehend, I experienced hell for 8 hours.

When I woke up again, I was told by the medical staff and praying Christians surrounding me that I had two surgeries lasting for many hours, and that I had regained consciousness after a total of 8 hours. The time I fell into hell seemed like a mere five to twenty minutes as I had lost all sense of time due to the pain I felt and the scene I saw. Nonetheless, the fear, pain, sorrow, and despair that the brief experience gave me was so great that I suffered from nightmares and its aftereffects for more than three months. The pain in hell was and is simply indescribable, something no human being should ever experience.

## JESUS CHRIST HIMSELF

Jesus Christ Himself spoke about this place of suffering called hell. I was there where the scorching fire never quenches and the worms do not die (Mark 9:48). I felt the burning heat and the horrors of the darkness myself, not to mention the utter despair. After this firsthand experience of the place that the words of the Bible describe, I am fully convinced and believe with all my heart that the words of Jesus are real and true regarding hell.

Before I opened my eyes again, I did not yet see Jesus Christ, but I heard a voice in my heart, a voice I have never heard before. He said, "No more Buddhism, no more drugs," and, "I love you." Unlike Buddha, this Spirit spoke to me.

When I woke up and opened my eyes, I immediately saw the pastors and prayer warriors who surrounded me at the hospital bed. They came to pray for me from a nearby Spirit-filled church called Grace Ministries International in Fullerton, California. At first, one of the prayer warriors looked into my eyes and said, "In Jesus' name, devil be gone!" I replied, "I am not the devil." Maybe they wanted to make sure I was not under any influence after what I did to myself.

I briefly described to them what I saw and experienced before I regained consciousness. They all replied that what I had just described is called hell. Then they immediately asked me if I wanted to pray the sinner's prayer. I said yes right away and remember repeating the prayer immediately. However, I did not feel any better or have peace, so I asked them, "Can I pray it again?" They said yes and led me in the same prayer to make Jesus my Lord and Savior one more time. Then I prayed it again. That day I prayed the sinner's prayer more than ten times after seeing hell and coming back.

At the time, I felt so fortunate and grateful to have been kept alive and concurrently felt the desperate need to pray that prayer because I was so afraid of the hell I had just seen. I never wanted to go back there ever again.

After praying the prayer, I did not become perfect right away, but I did renounce all other gods, religions, beliefs, and committed myself to Jesus alone for the salvation of my soul (John 14:6). After all, only His people came to help and pray for me when I needed help the most. It was Jesus' voice, not anyone else's, when I was in hell and came back. He saved me and showed me grace, love, and mercy by showing me the reality of hell as mentioned in the Bible.

Loving Christians from Grace Church continued to visit my home with baked goods, Bible study materials, and food to start discipleship with me at my home. I was still sick and recovering from the injuries of the failed suicide attempt, but God gave me enough strength to welcome them and sit up while they taught me the basic foundations of the Christian faith.

## GETTING AWAY

However, after that series of events and the accident, I needed to get away for a while. Around the beginning of November 1998, I went to local prayer retreat built by the same church, in Corona, California. I went with my family, except my dad who was in Korea at the time, to spend a few months growing in the faith and to recover physically.

At this Grace Prayer mountain retreat, they held services three times a day: 6 a.m., 11 a.m., and 8 p.m. I was so blessed to hear a man of prayer, the pastor who was the spiritual director there, named Pastor Jungsang Oh, lead service and preach three times daily, every day. He fasted 40 days in a row by drinking water only, and everyone called him the modern-day Moses because he always shared 10 spiritual points in every sermon.

While there, I heard people speaking in tongues, a spiritual prayer language mentioned in the New Testament of the Bible. I wanted this gift so badly but did not know how to receive it. I even became jealous of others who spoke and prayed in tongues. Then on November 20, 1998, Pastor Oh laid his hands on the top of my head, as he usually did after every 11 a.m. and 8 p.m. service, to bless us. That particular night, however, I felt fire go through my body and I received the gift of tongues. I will share more on this later in the book, but I felt so joyful and heavenly as I prayed like the other believers there in tongues and received God's calling and fire to see people repent, escape hell, and go to Heaven by the power of the name of Jesus and His Gospel alone! A new day and season had dawned upon me.

## A NEW DAY AND SEASON

I returned to school for the following spring semester in January 1999. After seeing hell and hearing the voice of Jesus and being baptized in the Holy Spirit, I thought I would become completely holy and perfect, but this was not the case.

My mother and younger brother became Christians after what they saw happen to me and hearing my accounts of hell, and they also received Jesus Christ. At school, I shared what happened to me, but only a handful repented and accepted Jesus. I went back to the same social group of partying friends on and off campus, but none of them wanted to hear the Gospel and asked why I still partied with them if I saw hell and became Christian. It was as if God was using even non-Christians to awaken me to live a holier life!

Others simply said, "Thank you for sharing your story," and did not receive Jesus. I did not know how to share the Gospel and my testimony at the time, but I tried my best. I was so grateful my family accepted Jesus, and now it was time to share the Gospel with my dad in Korea.

In the summer of 1999, I visited South Korea, where my dad was living at the time. Even after being saved and experiencing the grace of God, I began to party again when I went to Korea. I tried to become a Christian with all my heart. However, my friends from my former life who heard my testimony did not stop contacting me, and I partied even harder than before I met Jesus! I was bold because I had God but in a wrong way. I began to hang out with my old friends from high school in Korea again, drinking daily and partying, even after experiencing hell just 9 months prior. Though Jesus spoke to me at my neediest hour in life, I saw my life and heart had already turned away from Him—but my faithful Lord was not going to let me stay that way and head toward hell again.

## THE DREAM

In the middle of that summer, at the height of the daily drinking and partying in Korea, Jesus Christ appeared to me in a dream. God the Father Himself came as a light and spoke to me. I still vividly remember all the details. In that dream, I was standing on the top of a hill, and before my very eyes, the mountains, fields, and valleys stretched out so beautifully. I knew it was Heaven or the millennial kingdom. A heavenly, bright light shined in all directions. I clearly heard the voice of the Father God with my own ears. I even heard the heavenly choir of angels worshiping God and knew they were not human because no humanly choir could sing that beautifully.

The Lord God Himself spoke to me, "Jesus is my Son whom I love, and in Him I am well pleased. Listen to Him, listen to Him, listen to Him" (Matthew 17:5). When God speaks, He speaks His Word! I was so amazed and grateful to directly hear the audible voice of God, the Maker of Heaven and earth, the Maker of all human souls, King of kings and Lord of lords.

The scene in the dream was just like what the words of Revelation 21:2 (NKJV) describe: *"Then I, John, saw the holy city, New Jerusalem, coming down out of heaven from God, prepared as a bride adorned for her husband."* As these words came to life and translated into reality in my dream, there were angels praising the Lord on both sides of the light that enveloped the city, and I knew in my spirit it was the New Jerusalem. The voices of the angels were so sacred and beautiful that no human being could ever imitate them.

As of then, I had experienced both Heaven and hell by the grace of God. The pains of hell I had experienced compared to the warm and peaceful heavenly experiences of the heavenly Father are incomparable. I knew that the Lord desired to show me Heaven. This is mainly because the Lord wants all of His children to reach Heaven, each and every one. After seeing Heaven and audibly hearing God the Father's voice, I even felt a bit more healed from the trauma of seeing hell 9 months before.

These Heaven and hell experiences gave me a greater realization of the purpose of life, and that realization was enough to transform my life anew. Afterward, I made up my mind. I promised God and myself that I would share with others the experiences of Heaven and hell that God had shown me and I would convey to everyone I meet God's will, which is for all of His children to reach Heaven through faith in the Gospel (1 Timothy 2:4).

# 3

# THE REALITY OF HELL AND OTHER SIMILAR TESTIMONIES

Saint Teresa of Avila (not to be confused with Saint Teresa of Calcutta) is a well-known figure in Christian history who recorded her vision of hell. She was born in Avila, Spain, on March 28, 1515. She recorded her visit to hell in her autobiography:

> *One day while I was in prayer, I found myself all of a sudden transported entirely into Hell. I understood that God wanted me to see the place that the demons had prepared for me, and I that merited it with my sins. It was a vision of very little time, but it also lived on for many years, it seems I am not able to ever forget it. The entrance appeared to be a very long and narrow tunnel, similar to an oven very low, dark, and cramped; the soil was foul mud, full of filthy reptiles. In the distance, on the wall, there was a cavity carved out like a niche, and in it I felt tightly confined. And that which I then suffered exceeds every human imagination, nor does it seem possible to give even an idea because they are things which are indescribable. It is enough to know that how much I said, compared to the reality, makes it seem like a pleasant thing. I was feeling in my soul a fire that I do not know how to describe, while intolerable pains horrendously tore at my body. In my life I have suffered very much, some of the most serious, according to doctors, to undergo on earth, because my nerves were so contracted to the point of rendering me crippled, without saying the many others of various kinds, caused to me in part by the demon. Anyway, they*

*are not even able to be compared with how much I suffered at that time, especially that the thought of that torment would have had to be without end and without any mitigation. But even this was nothing in comparison to the agony of the soul. It was an oppression, an anguish, a sadness so profound, such a vivid and desperate pain that I do not know how to express myself. To say that they suffer continual agonies of death is inadequate, because at least in death, it seems that the life is ripped from others, whereas here, it is the same soul who makes himself into pieces. The fact is that I cannot find expressions to neither speak of that interior fire nor to make understandable the desperation which topped these horrible torments. I did not see who made me suffer them, but I felt myself burn and be lacerated, although the worst torment was the internal fire and desperation. It was a pestilential place, in which there was no longer any hope of comfort, nor space for one to sit or lay out, reinserted as I was in that hole made in the wall. Horrible to see oneself, the sides were weighing down upon me, and I felt as though suffocated. There was no light, but pitch black darkness; and as much as that could have given difficulty to sight one was able to see equally well regardless of the absence of light: something which I was not able to comprehend.*[1]

I can relate to Saint Teresa of Avila's vision of hell, and I am sure many others can as well who, by God's grace, were allowed to see hell in order to share of its reality with those who are still alive. When I was in hell for 8 hours in the fall of 1998, the feeling of hopelessness and despair, condemnation and guilt was unforgettable. I can tap into its memories when I try to recall. It is something I pray nobody feels or

1 *The Life of St. Teresa of Jesus,* Trans. David Lewis, September 27, 1094 (London: Thomas Baker) Online version at Project Gutenberg; http://www.gutenberg.org/ebooks/8120; accessed May 2, 2025.

experiences who is still alive on earth. The emotional pain there was 100 times worse than anything I felt on earth.

For me, the experience was more visual and spiritual than the other elements. More than the physical pain, though that was very painful, I remember the agony in my heart, and how I knew I would spend eternity there, and rightly so. I knew demons were gods there and that this punishment would never end.

What is hell? It is eternal separation from God. Is it a myth or reality? According to many and the words in the Bible and many other religions, it is definitely real—and the biggest lie of the devil is to tell you and all of humanity that it is not real.

Another person who wrote about hell whom I believe is authentic and with whom I can relate to is Bill Wiese. He wrote the book *23 Minutes in Hell,* and after his experience, went from being a real estate agent to a full-time evangelist. Praise God for his account. This is what he writes in the chapter titled, "The People I Saw in Hell":

> *In 1998 God gave me a life-changing vision of hell. I receive so many questions about my experience from people all over the world, but one question I'm often asked is, "Who did you see in hell?"*
>
> *There are others who say they've had a similar experience and go on to mention specific people they saw in hell. Some say they saw children and some say they encountered celebrities. Some also share that they observed Christians who didn't tithe, or women who wore jewelry or colored their hair. I saw none of this.*
>
> *In fact, none of those claims could be true because none of them are biblically accurate. People go to hell only because they reject the saving name of Jesus Christ. Choosing not to tithe will not send a person to hell. Jewelry, hair, makeup or any type of clothing will not send a person to hell. These outward acts are not the reason people go to hell.*

*The people I observed in hell looked like skeletons. They were nameless and faceless. I didn't know their history, their politics, or their skin color. I did not know if they were someone famous or a beggar from the streets. It didn't matter who they were; each of them was truly alone amidst a sea of tormented souls. They have no purpose, no identity, and they are forgotten.*

*I want to make very clear is that children are not in hell, according to the Bible. Jesus said in Matthew 19:14, "Suffer little children, and forbid them not to come unto me, for of such is the kingdom of heaven" (KJV). He also said in Matthew 18:3, "Except ye be converted, and become as little children, ye shall not enter the kingdom of heaven."*

*During my time in hell, I could see the outlines of people through the flames. From the outlines I saw that they seemed to be fully-grown or adult in size. In addition, the screams I heard were not the screams of children; they were mature voices. I will say that I also had an impression, an unexplainable internal feeling, that there were no children there.*

*As I look back on my experience, I'm reminded of the devastation of the twin towers of the World Trade Center on September 11, 2001. Rather than face the 2,000-degree heat, some people chose to plummet to their death by leaping out of a window. Those people chose to fall to their death rather than face the intensity of the flames for even fifteen seconds. According to the Bible, hell is deep down in the earth and scientists say it is 12,000 degrees. Try to imagine this state of existence for those in hell, and the fear that never ceases for even one second. This isn't just for 15 seconds, but for all eternity and there is no way to escape it.*

*To witness people in terror, in desperation, and in unending torment was more than I could bear. The questions I receive about*

> *who I saw in hell are so much less important than how these tormented souls ended up there.*[2]

Sometimes, the changes in life I see in the people who give their accounts of hell often convince me that their testimonies are true. Just as the disciples who walked with Jesus and saw His resurrection all laid down their lives for Him, so do those who see hell lay down their lives and comfort to lead one more soul away from hell to Jesus Christ and His Kingdom.

I can now say with complete confidence that I do not fall into depression or suicidal thoughts. Physical fatigue from overwork is not depression. But not taking care of one's body can lead to spiritual or emotional burnout. I am of the firm belief that we can feel true joy by loving and caring for our God-given body and spirit and that we can enjoy life to the fullest with Jesus, even on this side of Heaven.

If you are suffering from depression or lethargy right now, I say this: Take a moment to shift your standards of life away from yourself for a moment. Do you feel depressed when you are with other people? Do you feel sadness even when you are with God? Think about it. Perhaps when other people are around and you are more conscious of them, listening and looking into their lives, you won't have time for yourself to be depressed. You can notice the people in need around you, and you have a desire to help them. Find a way to help, and in that, the feeling of depression may disappear.

Jesus says in John 12:24 (ESV): *"Truly truly, I say to you, unless a grain of wheat falls into the earth and dies, it remains alone; but if it dies, it bears much fruit."* I am here to say that if one seed or self remains as it is, it is left alone. It is not good to be left alone. Conversely, as Jesus

---

2 Bill Wiese, "The Man Who Spent 23 Minutes in Hell: The People I Saw in Hell," *Charisma.com,* June 30, 2022; https://mycharisma.com/spiritled-living/the-man-who-spent-23-minutes-in-hell-the-people-i-saw-in-hell/; accessed April 12, 2025.

says, if you fall to the ground and die, you will bear much fruit. Dying to oneself to help others does not mean that you should turn away from or ignore your own ordeal of depression that is affecting you and always be with other people.

Rather, acknowledge the trials of depression, consciously focus on serving others, and try to be grateful to be alive. Sometimes people need psychiatric treatment as well to be cured of depression. I am not against medicine or drugs, because that is also one of the blessings the Lord has given humankind. But there is a limit to drug treatment, and the time will come when you will fully be healed by the Lord.

# 4

# OTHER RELIGIONS VERSUS CHRISTIANITY'S BELIEFS OF HELL[3]

For those who may not have a religious background or are unfamiliar with what major world religions believe about hell, I want to share some insights in this chapter to help you start exploring these very interesting differences for yourself. What you'll likely discover is that the concept of hell has been part of human history for most, if not all, of it. While we might think that modern advancements in science and civilization have made such ideas irrelevant, it's clear that death is inevitable for all humans, and God's Word remains unchanging through time.

Judaism has a traditional view on hell that can be found in the Tanakh (what Christians call the Old Testament). The Tanakh presents various images of God's final judgment on all mankind. A passage I often share when evangelizing or preaching is found toward the end of the book of Isaiah:

> *"For as the new heavens and the new earth which I will make shall remain before Me," says the Lord, "So shall your descendants and your name remain. And it shall come to pass that from one New Moon to another, and from one Sabbath to another, all flesh shall come to worship before Me," says the Lord. "And they shall go forth*

---

3 Some information in this chapter has been adapted from C.P. Ragland, Saint Louis University, "Hell," *Internet Encyclopedia of Philosophy (IEP)*, https://iep.utm.edu/hell/#H1; accessed April 12, 2025.

> *and look upon the corpses of the men who have transgressed against Me. For their worm does not die, and their fire is not quenched. They shall be an abhorrence to all flesh"* (Isaiah 66:22-24 NKJV).

Jesus often referred to the Old Testament in His teachings, and in the Gospel of Mark 9:48, He directly quotes this passage. In fact, some scholars argue that Jesus spoke more about hell than He did about Heaven. He describes hell as a place where *"their worm does not die, and the fire is not quenched."* Additionally, in Matthew 25:31-46, Jesus teaches about the final judgment where those who failed to care for the *"least of these"* will face *"eternal punishment"* in *"the eternal fire prepared for the devil and his angels."* Hell is also mentioned in Matthew 8:12, 22:13, 24:51, and 25:30.

Jesus went beyond the Old Testament descriptions, detailing hell as a place of *"outer darkness, where there will be weeping and gnashing of teeth."* In Luke 16:25-26 (NKJV), in the parable of the rich man and Lazarus, Jesus provides further clarity on the eternal nature of hell:

> *But Abraham said, "Son, remember that in your lifetime you received your good things, and likewise Lazarus evil things; but now he is comforted and you are tormented. And besides all this, between us and you* ***there is a great gulf fixed****, so that those who want to pass from here to you cannot, nor can those from there pass to us."*

The key point here is that hell is eternal. Once a soul is there, there is no escape. This is a stark contrast to the Catholic belief in purgatory, where people are taught they can temporarily suffer in hell, atone for their sins, and then eventually move on to Heaven. However, Jesus clearly taught that no one can cross from hell to Heaven, or vice versa. Hebrews 9:27 further reinforces this: *"It is appointed for men to die once, and after this the judgment."* This means that purgatory is a false teaching, even though it is widely believed by millions of people worldwide.

In today's postmodern world, many claim that truth is subjective. Regardless, Jesus taught that His Word is truth, and that truth brings life. This is where each person must make a choice: Will I trust in God's Word or follow man-made religious opinions? Let's be assured in our faith and choose to believe what God says about hell, rather than relying on human interpretations. It is not worth the gamble.

Finally, in the book of Revelation, the last book in the New Testament Christian Bible, God's Word also teaches us regarding the eternity of hell. In Revelation 20:7-15, we see that the devil, along with Death, Hades, and *anyone whose name was not found written in the book of life, cast into the lake of fire and sulfur...and they will be tormented day and night forever and ever.* Both the devil and unbelievers end up in hell, and the words *forever and ever* from God means exactly that, forever and ever. This is not a temporary punishment. If I were the devil and knew I was going there, a big lie I would make up to deceive people into coming with me would be tell them that hell is not real, or it is not eternal.

Even in Islam, the Quran teaches in many verses about hell, or *jahannam,* as a place of eternal blazing fire. It is referred to as "a prison-house" (17:8) in which "those who disbelieve and act unjustly... shall remain forever" (4:168). Again, it is both burning and forever. There people will "burn in hellfire. No sooner will their skins be consumed then God shall give them other skins, so that they may truly taste" divine wrath, again (4:55).

Buddhism also teaches that hell exists, but that it is temporary. As a former Buddhist disciple myself, I was taught reincarnation is true, or the belief that one's spirit is transferred to another newborn person's body, or even to an animal or insect. This is called the next-life in Buddhism.

Buddhism also teaches that some go to hell for a number of years, then come out, get reincarnated, die, and go to Heaven at times, only to return to earth. There were no solid principles nor guidelines. They believe that they are simply stuck in a perpetual cycle of life, death, reincarnation, hell, Heaven, and more next lives. The present life is a total sum of the blessings from good deeds, minus curses for bad deeds, of all the previous lives combined.

Unlike Christianity or Islam, hell is not eternal in Buddhism. Who created these spiritual laws in Buddhism? They do not know who, but it always has been that way, is the answer given for the 350 million Buddhists around the world.

I prefer the Bible's answer that God is the Maker of Heaven, earth, and hell; and as such, He Himself created the spiritual laws of life and death, and eternal punishment or rewards. Why should we be surprised that He who created the physical world, also created the spiritual world, and the laws?

The passages in both the book of Revelation and the Quran suggest that people in hell experience intense torment, aligning with the historical and traditional view of hell as a place of excruciating suffering. I once heard a renowned pastor from South Korea preach about hell, and he taught that the purpose of hell—created by a perfect God—is to perfectly avenge and punish those who failed to live faithfully according to His purposes. The concept of perfect punishment is eternal, not temporary. Even on earth, criminals who commit horrific acts like mass murder or torture are often sentenced to life in prison, sometimes multiple life sentences.

## AN ETERNAL AND LITERAL HELL

So, should we believe in an eternal and literal hell? According to the Word of God, we absolutely should. If hell were temporary or not real, we could live however we wanted on earth, committing all kinds of sins, and either pay for them in purgatory or work on improving ourselves in the next life. Then why repent and risk everything for God and others if hell is not real or eternal? Why are there Christian martyrs if hell is not real? On Judgment Day, the dead bodies of all who have ever lived will be resurrected, and the bodies of the unbelievers will be cast into a literal lake of fire (Revelation 20:12-14). Jesus says in the Bible that those who deny Him, He will deny before His Father in Heaven (Matthew 10:32-33).

Saint Augustine, an early church father who had a profound impact on many, wrote about both hell and Heaven. He said that the fire in hell will cause a physical agony that will burn but never consume the flesh of the damned, ensuring their torment never ends. Additionally, they will suffer psychologically, knowing that their most powerful desire, escaping hell, is impossible. This will lead them to experience not only frustration but utter despair. As Augustine put it, they will be "tortured with a fruitless repentance," filled with regret and self-loathing for their actions to not repent and believe in Jesus while on earth.

Some people argue that if God is love, hell cannot exist, or at least it is not a place of physical torment. They claim that the Bible's descriptions of eternal fire and darkness are symbolic or metaphorical, intended only to convey God's anger at humanity's sin. These individuals believe that God cannot or would not actually send anyone to hell because it contradicts the idea of a loving God. However, after reading the Bible numerous times and even experiencing hell myself in a near-death experience, I want to point out that this view stems from creating a god in our own image, a god that fits our preferences—rather than the holy God who created us.

The Bible is clear that God is not only loving but also holy. He is the holy, supreme God who punishes the wicked, as seen in passages including Psalm 11:5-6, Isaiah 13:11, and countless others. Jesus Christ, filled with both grace and truth (John 1:17), even referred to false religious leaders as "sons of the devil, snakes, brood of vipers, hypocrites," warning that the harshest judgment was reserved for them. Because Jesus is the Son of God, these words are true, and hell is not just a metaphor or scary image—it is a literal place where both the soul and body go after Judgment Day for the unbelievers.

## OUR LOVING GOD

So, does our loving God send people to hell?

First, I believe in free will and personal responsibility. Just like in all other areas of life, our choices have a profound impact on where we end up, whether in temporal matters or the most important question of all—where we end up after this life. The key to escaping hell and living life to the fullest here on earth is choosing to believe in and worship God through Jesus Christ (John 10:10).

Second, the Bible makes it clear that God desires all people to be saved and to spend eternity in Heaven (1 Timothy 2:4). Because God desires everyone to be saved, yet some choose to go to hell, it confirms the reality of free will. It is a choice that each individual makes. No one can blame God or anyone else for choosing hell for themselves.

In the chapters that follow, I share more about the interaction between humankind and God; but for now, I want to emphasize that most, if not all, major world religions believe in both hell and Heaven. And the choices we make matter, not only for eternity, but for this life as well.

"Annihilationism" is another non-Christian belief that goes against the teachings of the Bible. This view argues that the human soul ceases to exist in hell, essentially disintegrating or disappearing after death, forever. According to annihilationists, the souls of the saved will live forever, but the souls of the unsaved will be completely gone. Some proponents of annihilationism argue that a loving God would not send people to a place like hell, and so God must simply erase their existence.

However, this belief is flawed, as it has no support in the Bible or in any major religious texts throughout history.

Annihilationism stems from a misunderstanding of a traditional doctrine called divine conservation. This doctrine teaches that all created things depend on God to maintain their existence, meaning that things exist only as long as they are connected to God. In this flawed view, hell is seen as a state of non-existence, where people are permanently separated from God.

Nonetheless, the Bible clearly teaches otherwise. In Matthew 25:41 (NKJV), Jesus says: *"Then He will also say to those on the left hand, 'Depart from Me, you cursed, into the everlasting fire prepared for the devil and his angels.'"*

Hell was created for the devil and his angels, but anyone who chooses to follow the devil in their sin will also be cast there. Annihilationism, therefore, is one of the greatest lies ever introduced to humanity. It undermines the reality of eternal judgment and the significance of our choices in life.

The free will view, however, is far more in line with the biblical understanding of hell and why people go there. God created Adam and Eve, and all of humanity, to establish a love-based relationship with Him. However, love can only be genuine if both parties have the freedom to choose it. This is why God gives us free will, so we can choose to respond to His love. After 25 years of ministry and studying the Bible, I firmly believe that life makes the most sense when we understand that this life is temporary and that every human being is given the opportunity to accept or reject Jesus Christ.

## THE VALUE OF REPENTANCE

Throughout the Bible, we see the repeated pattern of humankind's disobedience. Adam and Eve sinned against God first, Israel repeatedly turned away from God throughout its history, and even the Church has fallen short by failing to live in full obedience to God. Yet, despite our failures, God is always the one who initiates reconciliation, through Jesus, the Holy Spirit, and His call to repentance. Repentance is not just feeling sorry for sin or saying a sinner's prayer; it means a complete change of mind and heart, especially regarding our relationship with God. It's about welcoming Him as King and embracing His Kingdom as the new set of values that govern our lives.

A person's heart is only big enough for one king, and repentance means allowing God to take full control of your heart. The fall of humankind, as described in Genesis 3:1-24, is a real and tragic event. And hell—eternal separation from God—is what every human being deserves, not Heaven. But the good news is that God, in His mercy, offers forgiveness and eternal life to all who choose to repent and accept Jesus as Lord.

On the other hand, universalism teaches that everyone ultimately deserves Heaven, and that nobody will go to hell. It suggests that there are many paths to Heaven and what's true for one person is true for another. This belief isn't specifically about hell, but more about why no one should go there. However, this view directly contradicts what God teaches in both the Old and New Testaments.

Universalism holds that all people will eventually be with God in Heaven. Some forms of universalism, like "necessary universalism," claim it is impossible for anyone to be eternally separated from God. Therefore, they argue, everyone must eventually be saved. While some universalists might say all people immediately go to Heaven after death, many try to align their beliefs with the Bible by suggesting that people will undergo a temporary period of post-mortem suffering (similar to purgatory in Catholicism) before entering Heaven. Again, this view does not align with the clear message of Scripture.

Are all truly saved? The answer, according to the Bible, is a definite "No." The Word of God teaches that more people will go to hell than to Heaven. Jesus makes this clear in Matthew 7:13-14 (ESV):

> *Enter by the narrow gate; for wide and the way is easy that leads to destruction, and those who enter by it are many. For the gate is narrow and the way is hard that leads to life, and those who find it are few.*

Jesus Himself tells us that the path to Heaven is narrow, and only a few will find it, while the wide path leads to destruction, and many walk on it. This is not just a theory; it is the reality that Jesus speaks about regarding eternity. Only those who are born again and repent of their sins will find the way to eternal life with God. Universalism simply does not line up with what Scripture teaches about salvation and the reality of hell.

## CHRISTIANITY AND OTHER RELIGIONS ON HELL

In many major world religions, hell is seen as a place of eternal torment for sinners, serving as one of two afterlife destinations, along with Heaven. As mentioned previously, in Islam, hell is called *jahannam,* described in the Quran as a place filled with fire and boiling water. In Hinduism, hell is known as *naraka,* but it is not considered a permanent destination. Instead, it is seen as a temporary place where people pay for the wrongs they committed in past lives, before being reborn. Buddhism shares a similar concept, emphasizing the cycle of rebirth and the opportunity for eventual escape from suffering, which directly contradicts Jesus' teachings on hell.

Interestingly, Judaism does not have a clear concept of hell today, but it does have the idea of the apostate, someone who renounces God and His ways, and is considered "cut off" from the covenant community.

Despite all these alternative beliefs, which often contradict God's Word, the Bible remains clear: hell is real, and it is eternal.

The reality of hell is entirely compatible with the existence of a just and loving God. A loving and just God must punish evil while offering salvation to those who repent. The concept of hell aligns with God's mercy, as the Bible teaches that He gives every person free will. People choose whether to follow God or reject Him, and this choice ultimately determines their eternal destiny. God desires all people to be saved, but not everyone chooses to accept that invitation.

So, is there any sin or collection of sins that truly deserves eternal punishment? Yes, it is the rejection of God.

I was taken by surprise during my time in Toronto, Canada, by conversations I had with people who openly stated that they did not need or want a God who loved them, and the same people dismissed God, as according to them, He was made up for "weak" individuals to be their crutch. What they fail to realize is that every person, regardless of how strong or independent they seem now, will eventually face the reality of aging and death. It is impossible for anyone to remain strong forever. How can such people expect Heaven to be their eternal home when they reject the very God who created it and dwells there?

Now, you might ask, is free will really compatible with an all-powerful and all-knowing God? Because God is truly omnipotent and omniscient, why does He not simply force everyone to repent and choose Heaven? The answer lies in the nature of God's power and His respect for free will. God, in His infinite wisdom and love, allows people to choose their eternal fate. He did not make Adam and Eve sin in the Garden of Eden. He did not force their decision. God is not a masochist who delights in tormenting humanity. He does not tempt anyone, nor is He tempted, as the Bible states in James 1:13-14 (NIV):

> *When tempted, no one should say, "God is tempting me." For God cannot be tempted by evil, nor does he tempt anyone; but each person is tempted when they are dragged away by their own evil desire and enticed.*

Additionally, in Galatians 6:7-8 (NIV) we read:

> *Do not be deceived: God cannot be mocked. A man reaps what he sows. Whoever sows to please their flesh, from the flesh will reap destruction; whoever sows to please the Spirit, from the Spirit will reap eternal life.*

Here, *"flesh"* refers to our sinful nature, while *"Spirit"* refers to the new nature of a person who is born again and led by the Spirit of God. The *"destruction"* spoken of is eternal separation from God, hell. The *"eternal life"* refers to Heaven. Both Heaven and hell are very real, and both have been a fundamental belief of the Church since its inception.

The purpose of this book is to open your eyes to the reality of hell, to urge you to repent, and to surrender your life to the Jesus of the Bible, the only Son of God, so that you can have eternal life in Heaven. The book of Acts shows us exactly how to repent and receive eternal life, right here and now. It is not just about a future destination; it is about a relationship with God that transforms your life today.

In Acts 2:22-41 (ESV), we see very clearly how Jesus Christ overcame death and hell. We also see Peter calling all listeners to hear, repent, and live, even live forever!

> *"Men of Israel, hear these words: Jesus of Nazareth, a man attested to you by God with mighty works and wonders and signs that God*

*did through him in your midst, as you yourselves know—this Jesus, delivered up according to the definite plan and foreknowledge of God, you crucified and killed by the hands of lawless men. God raised him up, loosing the pangs of death, because it was not possible for him to be held by it.*

*"For David says concerning him, 'I saw the Lord always before me, for he is at my right hand that I may not be shaken; therefore my heart was glad, and my tongue rejoiced; my flesh also will dwell in hope. For you will not abandon my soul to Hades, or let your Holy One see corruption. You have made known to me the paths of life; you will make me full of gladness with your presence.'*

*"Brothers, I may say to you with confidence about the patriarch David that he both died and was buried, and his tomb is with us to this day. Being therefore a prophet, and knowing that God had sworn with an oath to him that he would set one of his descendants on his throne, he foresaw and spoke about the resurrection of the Christ, that he was not abandoned to Hades, nor did his flesh see corruption. This Jesus God raised up, and of that we all are witnesses. Being therefore exalted at the right hand of God, and having received from the Father the promise of the Holy Spirit, he has poured out this that you yourselves are seeing and hearing.*

*"For David did not ascend into the heavens, but he himself says, 'The Lord said to my Lord, "Sit at my right hand, until I make your enemies your footstool." Let all the house of Israel therefore know for certain that God has made him both Lord and Christ, this Jesus whom you crucified.'"*

*Now when they heard this they were cut to the heart, and said to Peter and the rest of the apostles, "Brothers, what shall we do?"* ***And Peter said to them, "Repent and be baptized every one of you in the name of Jesus Christ for the forgiveness of your***

***sins, and you will receive the gift of the Holy Spirit. For the promise is for you and for your children and for all who are far off, everyone whom the Lord our God calls to himself."*** *And with many other words he bore witness and continued to exhort them, saying, "Save yourselves from this crooked generation." So those who received his word were baptized, and there were added that day about three thousand souls.*

# 5

# BORN-AGAIN CHRISTIANS VS. FALSE CHRISTIANS

## THROUGH FALSE REPENTANCE OF CONTINUAL UNGODLY LIFESTYLES

I never thought "Christians" could go to hell, until I started digging deeper into the Scriptures. Around 2008, I met a pastor at a revival in California who completely shifted my perspective. His name is Pastor Boyoung Park, and he is my favorite pastor out of all the 55,000 Protestant Korean churches that exist today. What makes him stand out is his testimony and faith life story. He grew up in a family of pastors: his grandfather, father, uncles, aunts, and even brothers were all pastors, except him. Why? He saw so much division and fighting in the churches where his family served. He believed God was dead and Christianity was fake. Jesus' disciples could only live such lives because He is not real, was his conclusion.

As a result, Pastor Park chose a different path. He became a medical doctor in his 30s and married into an affluent non-Christian family. Then when he hit his late 30s, he was diagnosed with an incurable heart disease and was given only a few months to live. Knowing his own prognosis, he finally went to a prayer mountain that his uncle led. A prayer mountain is like a modern-day monastery or retreat where people go to pray, fast, and reflect.

While there, Pastor Park had a life-changing encounter with God. He was miraculously healed of his heart condition—and during the Christmas season, he gave his life to Jesus. He sold or gave everything he had to the poor and spent 10 years literally living among the homeless people. After those 10 years, Jesus visited him again, this time to launch him into one of the most influential and deeply devout ministries in Korea. Since then, he has planted some of the healthiest, most Spirit-filled churches I have ever seen, all rooted in solid biblical teaching.

I could share so much more about him, but I want to focus on a powerful vision that Jesus gave him, which directly ties into what we are discussing in this book. In the vision, Pastor Park saw countless people walking toward a cliff. They were all wearing one of three types of clothing. At the edge of the cliff was a steep drop into flames—hell. Half the people were dressed in black clothes, the other half in gray, and only a few scattered here and there wore white.

Pastor Park wanted to ask Jesus what the different colors meant, but before he could speak, Jesus answered him. He explained that those in black were nonbelievers—people who never acknowledged or accepted Christ, and they were walking straight into eternal hell. The people in gray were those who went to church, listened to sermons, and played the part of a Christian, but never truly repented. They were religious, but never experienced a personal, intimate relationship with Jesus. Despite looking like Christians to others, they too were heading straight for hell.

Finally, the people in white clothes were those who had truly been washed by the blood of Jesus. They had repented, surrendered their lives to Christ, and served His Kingdom with everything. These were the born-again believers—those who had truly given their lives to Jesus. While they were few, they were the ones who were taken up into Heaven by a powerful light, spared from the cliff and the flames below.

The question for you today—what color are you wearing?

## HEAVEN ENCOUNTER CONFERENCE

God loves me so much that He sent me to be a featured speaker at the very first "Heaven Encounter Conference" held in October 2024, in San Diego, California. Pastor Randy Kay and his wife, Renee, hosted the event and flew in speakers from all over, though I drove from nearby Orange County. At the conference, I met a dozen other believers who had experienced near-death experiences, hell, Heaven, and Jesus Christ. Some had even more extreme encounters than I had.

One of the featured speakers was Retha McPherson, a Spirit-led speaker from South Africa. She's the author of *The New York Times* bestseller *Message from God*, where she shares her inspiring story about losing her son, Aldo, in a traumatic car accident. Aldo entered Heaven, met Abraham, Moses, and Jesus Christ, and then miraculously returned to share his visit. What is truly amazing is that Aldo had the exact same vision of the three types of people that Pastor Boyoung Park had. Had Pastor Park and Aldo ever met? I seriously doubt it.

For one, Pastor Park does not speak English and lives in South Korea, while Aldo and Retha are from South Africa and do not speak Korean. They are miles apart in language and culture. But despite that, their stories align, showing us that hell is real, many people are heading there, but anyone who repents and lives a surrendered life to Christ can go to Heaven and experience God's love, both here on earth and for eternity.

Is it an easy life to live with and for God? I would say no, but honestly, it is much harder to live without God, both here on earth and for all of eternity. Through faith in the Cross, you can let Jesus live through you, and not remain a religious person striving for acceptance and trying to earn salvation from God. Allow Jesus Christ to love on you and live in you.

God loves you deeply. You have to surrender and receive that love, though. God loves me, and I truly believe I am His favorite child. Just think about it. John 15:9 (NIV) says, *"As the Father has loved me, so have I loved you. Now remain in my love."* How much does God the Father love Jesus, His Son? As His favorite. And because of that, it is now only logical to say that you are Jesus' favorite, and therefore God's favorite, too!

## REAL, BIBLICAL CHRISTIANITY

What exactly is real, biblical Christianity? You have a human right to know. Someone should have shared it with you clearly. If not, I apologize on your Christian or neighbor's behalf.

Christianity is all about God's Son, Jesus, who is both fully God and fully Man. We were made in God's image, created for His glory and fellowship. As His stewards, His representatives on earth, especially in the Garden of Eden, we were designed to walk with God in perfect freedom, without shame. We were free to do everything except eat from the tree of the knowledge of good and evil. That was the one command God gave us. The Gospel is something that all Christians and seekers alike must clearly understand.

Satan, the devil, came into the Garden and lied to Eve, and through her, to Adam, and to us. On the day we disobeyed God, we died. We did not become more enlightened; instead, our eyes were opened to shame, guilt, and a deep separation from God. We did not become like God, we became cursed. The serpent, satan, knew that God knew good and evil. However, when we ate from the tree of knowledge, we did not gain wisdom, but confusion. We inherited a distorted understanding of good and evil, not godly knowledge.

Due to Adam and Eve's disobedience, the entire world was cursed. God views our decision to eat from the tree as a direct act of rebellion, as a desire to take His place. It is a great offense to God, though it might seem small to us. We are made in His image, but we are not God. God is the Creator, and no matter how great we think we are, we are still the created, not the Creator. God is the Master, and we are His servants. He is our Father, and if we believe in Jesus, we are His children.

The tree of knowledge of good and evil in the center of the Garden represented the boundary God set as King, Creator, and God. When we think we can become or replace Him, we become enemies of God, and that ends the relationship between us and God. This separation is the literal and biblical definition of death. Yes, there is physical death, but the more terrifying death is when we lose our relationship with God and are separated from Him. Many are born into this world physically, but unless they are truly born again, they remain spiritually dead, out of right relationship with God.

Buddhism, and many other religions, teach that life is about self-existence and self-realization. As a former Buddhist, I can tell you how sincere, yet misguided, these beliefs can be. Buddhism teaches that we can become gods and pay for our sins through endless prayer. However sin, according to God, is what separates us from Him. The result of sin is false religions, misconceptions about how to reach Heaven, and the fear of hell.

## THE CONSEQUENCES OF SIN

So what exactly is sin? What are its effects on humanity, both individually and corporately? Romans 6:23 (NIV) says, *"For the wages of sin is death, but the free gift of God is eternal life through Christ Jesus our Lord."* Sin always says, "Give me, give me, give me," and it leads to death. But God says, "Take from Me, take from Me, take from Me," and it leads to eternal life.

A person who sins is always trying to take from others, and they die on the inside. God is the opposite. He always gives, and He is full of love and life. What an amazing God we can approach at any time of day or night! He says, "Come to Me." The invitation of the Bible is summed in one word, *come!* Come and see, come and receive forgiveness, come and be healed, come and be united with God, come and find rest and true joy, love that quenches all desires and thirsts in your soul.

Everyone who comes to God, obeys God, believes in Him, and lives for Him will change according to their God-given purpose and calling. Believers are ready to love, give, and serve others. And in doing so, God's eternal life flows through them and they grow and mature. When you become a man or woman of God, you naturally want to love and give without striving because you carry the new nature of Christ within you.

However on the other hand, someone who tries to become god needs more and more to fill the emptiness and is dying spiritually. The worst thing in life is to become your own god; and the best thing in life is when you make Jesus your Lord, you walk in eternal life and share that life with everyone you meet. When I try to be my own god, I lose everything. But when I accept Jesus, God Himself gives me everything—life, redemption, and eternity.

## THE POWER OF REDEMPTION

John 17:3 says *eternal life is knowing the only true God, and Jesus Christ whom He has sent.* When we repent, we are redeemed. To *redeem* means to buy something back, to repay. Spiritually speaking, God bought us back from sin and death. Satan tricked us into thinking we could become gods; but in reality, we became slaves—slaves to sin, to the devil, and to our own selfish desires. God created us to be free, but sin brought us into bondage. In sin, we feel anxious, empty, and constantly seeking something to fill that void.

The Gospel tells us that God came to satan and said, "These are My children." Satan replied, "No, they're mine. You have to buy them back." And that is what Romans 6:23 means. There was a price to pay to redeem us from sin and death. What can pay for death? Meditation? Good deeds? More money, bitcoins? It has to be something of equal or greater value. And that is exactly what Jesus did for us. He gave His life in exchange for ours.

Jesus Christ paid the price for us, redeeming us from eternal death. This is something we can understand in simple terms. God decided to redeem us by sending His Son, Jesus Christ. God never sold us to satan. We betrayed Him of our own free will. Christianity is about trusting that Jesus saves us from our sins. Salvation is redemption. We are bought back to God through the death and resurrection of Jesus Christ. It's free to us, but it was costly to Jesus—He paid for our sins with His life.

Through Jesus, we are forgiven, redeemed, righteous, blameless, sinless, and guilt-free—once and for all. This is amazing grace. The Gospel is all about redemption! How do we receive this redemption? By repenting sincerely, with all our heart, and trusting in Jesus Christ and His Word. Salvation is a gift, but it is a gift that comes, came, at a great cost, the cost of Jesus' life.

Then, why do some religious Christians still go to hell? They do so because they never truly learned the meaning of Christianity in their hearts. They do not understand who Jesus is, the meaning of His name, or the true nature of their own sins and its effects. They have not experienced the power of redemption but simply attended church. They are born but not born-again. Only God can pay for our sins. That is why He sent His Son, Jesus, to redeem us. Now we can return to God, free from the power of sin and death.

Redemption is what God did for us. We cannot please Him through our own works or striving. Our part is to trust Him, surrender to Him, and enjoy His presence. This is the amazing grace of the biblical Gospel!

It is all about the Cross of Christ! Let Jesus Christ live through you; and as you walk in His grace, share His life with everyone you meet.

## WHAT THE NEW TESTAMENT SAYS ABOUT JESUS AND HIS PEOPLE, THE CHURCH

Ephesians reminds us that we are in Jesus Christ, through His grace, and by His blood, as shown in chapter 1. We've been forgiven of our sins and redeemed because Jesus Christ is in us, sent by God Himself. Hebrews 9:27 reminds us that God judges everyone, but Jesus was offered once and for all to bear the sins of many, and we eagerly await His second coming.

Leviticus 17:11 shows us that without the shedding of blood, there is no forgiveness of sins. In the Old Testament, the blood of animals temporarily dealt with sin, but it all pointed to the ultimate sacrifice of Jesus Christ, who would shed His own blood to redeem us once and for all. Now, we can live for God as fully loved and accepted children, because Jesus finished the work of salvation for us. God declares us righteous!

Because of Jesus' sacrifice, we are no longer enemies of God, but we are righteous in His sight. The Father is fully pleased with us through His Son, Jesus Christ, because He redeemed us on the Cross, and now He can save anyone who believes. This is the righteousness of God. Right and wrong are not defined by human standards; right and wrong are defined by God, who is righteous and holy.

Our human perspective on good and evil cannot save us, but God's standard is eternal and perfect. Only the eternal Holy Spirit can bring us true, lasting joy, and understanding of everything that comes from God and Jesus Christ. We cannot save ourselves or gift ourselves with joy or life. It can only come from God! Surrender is the key. Obeying when God commands, speaking and acting when He tells us to. That is when miracles happen and God's grace is evident. This is the normal Christian life! As we see ourselves the way God sees us, we grow in our faith, and this is what defines maturity in Christ.

## JESUS SAVES

The sacrifice of Jesus on the Cross was prophesied in Isaiah 53, 700 years before His birth. This passage paints a picture of the Triune God's conversation to save humankind. The Trinity: God the Father, God the Son, and God the Holy Spirit are one. The name *Jesus* means "He saves."

To understand sin today, we need to clarify what it truly is. Sin is "missing the mark" in Greek, and in Hebrew it means "failing or missing the goal." Sin is failing God. Sin is anything God calls sin, not what we call sin.

Isaiah 53 focuses on Jesus' sacrifice to redeem us and shows how He alone is eternal life. His blood alone can save us forever. Jesus worked with the Holy Spirit to accomplish this, and the Triune God planned it long before Jesus came to earth. The Father asked the Son to be stricken, afflicted, and wounded to redeem us back to Him. Just like Abraham was called to offer Isaac, God Himself prepared the sacrifice, Jesus, to reconcile us to Himself. Before the foundation of the world, the Father asked His Son to lay down His life for our redemption.

In Gethsemane, Jesus was praying earnestly, with blood-like sweat, asking that the cup of suffering might pass from Him. The suffering felt by one person of the Triune God is felt by all Three. Isaiah 53 reflects this conversation between the Father, Son, and Holy Spirit as they decided that Jesus would pay the ultimate price for us, His very own life.

When we encounter the Holy Spirit, we begin to understand that God's Word is alive and active, working here and now, not just in the past. God's Word isn't bound by time or space. It works in the present moment as we read, pray, and proclaim it. We also need the Holy Spirit to help us believe in the reality of Heaven and hell—it's called conviction.

The crucifixion of Jesus is not just a past event. It has effects that continue to save people now. The righteousness of God can be ours today by faith. Those who please God are righteous, and those who do not are wicked. Human standards of right and wrong are temporary and relative, but God's commandments are eternal. We may wonder how such a good person could go to hell, but our judgment of others doesn't matter. Only God, who judges perfectly, can determine who is righteous. Obedience is greater than sacrifice.

First Peter 3:19-20 reveals that Jesus, in His Spirit, went to hell to preach to the souls there from the days of Noah. No one knows exactly what He preached, but as the obedient Son, He went, and the disobedient souls remained in prison (hell). Jesus, filled with grace and truth, is the obedient One who obeyed God and is the reason we can now be righteous. Christians are no longer just good people. They are righteous, empowered by the Holy Spirit to carry out God's will. Just as Jesus submitted Himself to the Father, even to the point of death, we are called to submit to God, to obey, and to serve. Those who do not obey God do not enter Heaven, but those who do are welcomed.

One of my favorite images in Christendom is the painting of Jesus praying in Gethsemane. I have a framed copy of it in my bedroom. In His prayer, we see Jesus fulfilling the prophecy of Isaiah 53, the fulfillment of God's requirement for all people to be made righteous. Jesus Christ, through His obedience, laid down His life on the Cross to offer redemption for all who believe. Second Corinthians 5:17-21 (NKJV) says:

> *Therefore, if anyone is in Christ, he is a new creation; old things have passed away; behold, all things have become new. Now all things are of God, who has reconciled us to Himself through Jesus Christ.... We are ambassadors for Christ, as though God were pleading through us: we implore you on Christ's behalf, be reconciled to God. For He made Him who knew no sin to be sin for us, that we might become the righteousness of God in Him.*

This means that anyone in Christ becomes a peacemaker, an ambassador to the Kingdom of God, bringing reconciliation between God and humankind through Jesus Christ and the Gospel. It's important to understand the Trinity: God the Father, Son, and Holy Spirit are three equal persons, co-equal in glory and majesty, united as one. They existed before time and will exist forever.

Jesus came to earth during Passover to pay for sins once and for all. Just as in the Exodus, where the blood of the lamb saved the Israelites, Jesus' blood covers our sins, not just for the Jews, but for all people and all generations.

Jesus' death and resurrection, just as Jonah spent three days in the whale, was the sign to save all generations. Jesus is our faithful Husband who marries the Church, resurrecting Israel (the Church) through His sacrifice. Jesus came to Jerusalem, the city of peace, and paid for sins with His blood, bringing peace for all who believe. Jesus is the ultimate Sacrifice, and the need for animal sacrifices in the Old Testament is gone. Now, we surrender to Jesus and walk the narrow road of life, avoiding hell and receiving the gift of eternal life.

Hebrews 10:10-14 explains that we've been sanctified through the offering of Jesus' body, once and for all. Priests in the Old Testament offered sacrifices repeatedly, but Jesus offered one sacrifice for sins forever, sitting down at the right hand of God. He perfected forever those who are being sanctified.

Even after we are saved and become part of the true Jerusalem, the bride of Christ, we will face attacks from satan. Regardless, we daily carry our cross, resist the devil, and submit to God. The purpose of Christianity is not just to avoid hell, it is also to enjoy God, obey Him, and be His children. We do not strive to figure things out, but we surrender and obey His will. If you have not surrendered to Jesus Christ and obeyed His commands, you might not have assurance of salvation. Now is the time to repent, surrender your life fully to God, and be 100 percent sure of your place in Heaven when you die. You too can avoid hell for all of eternity. In later chapters, I will share more on what a surrendered life looks like.

## WHERE DID OTHER WORLD RELIGIONS COME FROM?

There are two kinds of people in this world: those who have religion and those who do not. Among those who follow religion, there are two groups: those who are born again and those who are not. We can divide humanity into those who believe in God's existence and those who do not. Those who believe in God see everything as created by Him, and those who do not hold that view. We are talking about atheism here, but we also know that many false religions have sprung up, claiming that there are many roads to Heaven.

When we talk about religion, we can say that humans are inherently religious. We have been created to worship. Even atheists, in rejecting the idea of God, end up with their own belief system. Atheism itself becomes a kind of religion. When comparing Christianity to other religions, it is important to remember that it is unique. Christianity cannot be lumped together with other religions, because it stands apart due to the nature of its belief system.

So how did other religions come about? Some people are naturally more thoughtful and inquisitive. They have sought God, trying to find a way to connect with Him, and religions are often seen as the result of these efforts and ideas. The Bible provides us with an early example of this in the story of Cain and Abel, the offspring of Adam and Eve. Both Cain and Abel were raised by Adam and Eve, and they both had a desire to approach God. It is admirable to have a heart that seeks God, but their ways of approaching Him could not have been more different, and the outcomes were worlds apart.

Cain tried to seek God on his own terms. He thought that just as one might knock on a neighbor's door, he could approach God however he liked. He figured that since he was offering something, God would be pleased. He probably believed he was well-prepared and that his offering would make God happy. It is an attitude you will find in many religions. People think they can approach God by their own standards, believing that offering something, whether it is time, good deeds, or rituals, they will please God more.

However, God does not accept offerings that are not in line with His will. Cain's way of thinking was flawed, and as a result, his offering was rejected. This led to his anger and, tragically, murdering his brother, Abel. Abel, on the other hand, offered God what He asked for and pleased Him. Cain's story is a clear example of how man-made ways of approaching God will never lead to true salvation.

## HUMAN PRIDE AND FUTILE PURSUIT

In the same way, the attempt to build the Tower of Babel is a picture of human pride and the futile pursuit of reaching Heaven through human effort. After the flood, the descendants of Noah's sons, Shem, Ham, and Japheth, decided to build a tower that reached the heavens. The Bible does not say exactly how tall the Tower of Babel was, but it was likely enormous. It might have been taller than the Great Pyramids or the Great Wall of China, structures that were impressive in their own right.

Nevertheless, despite their grand scale, the tower was still nothing more than an earthly structure, a human effort to reach the divine. The builders thought they could connect Heaven and earth through their work, but this was nothing more than human pride, trying to reach God through their own creations.

The Tower of Babel is a symbol of all religions and human-made efforts to reach God. No matter how grand the plans or the blueprints, if they come from human minds, they are still just like the Tower of Babel: futile, finite, and ultimately powerless. Humanity's attempts to create ways to God after the fall in Eden are like trying to leap toward Heaven but only falling short, like fleas trying to jump to the moon. The truth is that no human-made religion or effort will ever bridge the gap between us and God. Only the way God has provided will lead us to Him. We know Jesus is the only way to Heaven according to John 14:6.

When we see fleas jumping dozens or even hundreds of times, they might think it is an impressive feat, but from our perspective, it is nothing. In the same way, God looks at human efforts to reach Him through religion and He laughs. No matter how hard we try, there is no way for us to approach God on our own terms. Some people even retreat to monasteries, cut off from the world, believing that by removing themselves from distractions, they can purify themselves and become more like God. They deceive themselves into thinking that by training their bodies and minds, they can transcend their sinful nature. Nonetheless, this is a delusion.

This is why many religions were created by people who withdrew from society and spent time in isolation, in nature or the mountains, trying to become more spiritual. They believed that by doing so, they could achieve a higher state of being. However, these attempts are ultimately human inventions, and when you step back and think about it, they are actually quite ridiculous.

This is why we see so many religions springing up all around the world, like bamboo shoots after a rainstorm. In South Korea alone, there are over 100,000 self-proclaimed messiahs or cult leaders. People in different regions and cultures have created religions based on their own ideas, hoping to find or become gods. And this trend continues, giving rise to countless superstitions.

God created us to be thinking, rational beings because we are made in His image. It is clear that world religions were not divinely revealed but were the product of human thought. Many people live as if this life is all there is, simply eating, sleeping, and going through the motions. The more intellectual ones, however, have created religions in an attempt to understand life and its purpose. Yet, too often, people blindly accept these beliefs without ever questioning them. True faith is not about blindly following; it is about thinking critically and searching for truth. That is why many people, in their pursuit of rationality and real faith, reject all world religions and superstitions.

However, most people are still spiritual or religious in some way. Even those who do not consciously seek God often find themselves grasping at anything that can provide comfort, especially in moments of crisis. This is why superstitions and false religions continue to grow, giving people temporary emotional relief. However, no matter how spiritual or lofty a religion appears, if it comes from human minds, it is just another imitation. It may provide some comfort and security for a time, but it will not lead to salvation. It cannot keep anyone from hell if it is simply an attempt to reach God on our own terms.

And that is what all man-made religions are. They are not divine. They may look spiritual, even offer some emotional satisfaction, but they are human creations, and therefore false. The truth is this: anything created by human beings is not divine, and therefore is not a true religion. It is simply superstition. Nothing more, nothing less.

Christianity, on the other hand, is different. It is not a man-made religion. It is a revealed religion, revelation. It comes from God Himself. The belief system of Christianity teaches us how to avoid hell and how to live in a way that is worthy of the Gospel and the sacrifice of Jesus' blood. When we begin to reject the lies of man-made religions and embrace the truth of the Gospel, we prove to ourselves, to God, and to our own consciences that we are truly on the path to Heaven.

You do not go to Heaven because you are a good person. If this is true, then Jesus Christ died for nothing, and there is no need for the Cross. Breaking one sin makes a sinner, and we are all born sinners. The truth is not fair. It is a Person, Jesus Christ.

# 6

# BIBLE VERSES ON HELL, AND HOW TO AVOID GOING THERE

## WITH GOD'S SPIRIT, SURRENDER TO HIM!

I have been in ministry since 2004, starting as a pastor intern. Before that, I had the privilege of living in China where I shared the Gospel with as many people as I could. I graduated from the University of California, Irvine, in 2003, and during my time there, I proudly carried my Bible around and witnessed many people come to Jesus Christ.

In the spring of 2004, I started at Talbot School of Theology in La Mirada, California. With God's help, I graduated in 2008, and I am incredibly grateful that I had the opportunity to study the Bible more deeply, including Greek, Hebrew, and theology. It was a season of growth that shaped my understanding and passion for God's Word. Studying, however, needs to be applied, meaning we must serve others and save the lost using the knowledge gained at school and the wisdom gained from the Bible.

After I was saved from hell, God spoke to me very clearly. He told me to share Jesus with just one more soul. And so whether on the streets, in churches, gyms, theaters, Walmarts, restaurants, and even mosques, I go out and preach His Gospel. In 2024 alone, God had me preach at more than 90 church events and interviews, sharing my testimony of seeing both hell and Heaven. That does not include the daily prayer meetings or the weekly evangelism events we have. Whether in a podium, on YouTube, in the streets, or to our friends and coworkers, we preach Jesus, and His Cross. Some of these events last for days, with preaching required day and night, at retreat centers up in the mountains.

As I preach about Heaven and hell to so many people, I have noticed something powerful: I see a stronger response to the call of repentance when I talk about hell, more than when I just speak about Heaven. It is as if the reality of eternity hits harder when people understand the consequences of rejecting God. Of course, Jesus Himself taught us about hell, especially through the parable in the Gospel of Luke, which has become my favorite Gospel to read nowadays. In Luke 16:19-31 (ESV), we see Jesus teaching us the parable of the rich man and beggar Lazarus:

> *There was a rich man who was clothed in purple and fine linen and who feasted sumptuously every day. And at his gate was laid a poor man named Lazarus, covered with sores, who desired to be fed with what fell from the rich man's table. Moreover, even the dogs came and licked his sores. The poor man died and was carried by the angels to Abraham's side. The rich man also died and was buried, and in Hades, being in torment, he lifted up his eyes and saw Abraham far off and Lazarus at his side. And he called out, "Father Abraham, have mercy on me, and send Lazarus to dip the end of his finger in water and cool my tongue, for I am in anguish in this flame." But Abraham said, "Child, remember that you in your lifetime received your good things, and Lazarus in like manner bad things; but now he is comforted here, and you are in anguish. And besides all this, between us and you a great chasm has been fixed, in order that those who would pass from here to you may not be able, and none may cross from there to us." And he said, "Then I beg you, father, to send him to my father's house—for I have five*

> *brothers—so that he may warn them, lest they also come into this place of torment." But Abraham said, "They have Moses and the Prophets; let them hear them." And he said, "No, father Abraham, but if someone goes to them from the dead, they will repent." He said to him, "If they do not hear Moses and the Prophets, neither will they be convinced if someone should rise from the dead."*

Here we see a rich man, whose name is not even mentioned, living a lavish life every day, completely ignoring the beggar Lazarus who sat at his gate. Lazarus was so poor that he couldn't even get the scraps that fell from the rich man's table. Both men died, and their fates were drastically different. Lazarus was taken to Heaven, while the rich man went to hell.

In hell, the rich man, in his torment, saw Lazarus with Abraham in Heaven and begged for just a drop of water to cool his tongue. But Abraham's response, reflecting God's message, was clear: people need to listen to the Scriptures, to the words of the Bible, while they are still alive. *"Moses and the Prophets"* refers to the Old Testament (or the Tanakh in Hebrew), and it all points to Jesus Christ. John 5:39 (ESV) makes this crystal clear: *"You search the Scriptures because you think that in them you have eternal life; and it is they that bear witness about me."* Every person who repents after hearing the truth of the Bible, the Gospel, has the opportunity to go to Heaven and avoid hell. We have to repent and choose life while we are alive, not after death.

Miracles are part of how God draws us to believe, but even they are not the end goal in themselves. Rather, they point us to the true miracle-maker, Jesus Christ Himself. In this story about the rich man and Lazarus, we can draw four spiritual truths about life, death, and eternity:

1. God sends people to hell who do not repent.
2. We will go to hell or to Heaven after death.

3. We should listen to God's Word and repent now, and warn others to do the same.
4. We should not neglect to tell others.

There are only three types of people in the world, according to the Word of God. From God's perspective, these categories are clear: 1) Those who are in the flesh (the natural man, not yet repented); 2) Those who are in the fleshly nature (carnal, still needing to repent); and 3) Those who are in the Spirit (spiritual or in Jesus Christ). There are no other types from God's view, as laid out in the Scriptures. First Corinthians chapters 2 and 3 teach this truth clearly and plainly.

The first type of person is the unbeliever, or non-Christian. The other two types are both churchgoers or Christians. However, those who are still walking in the flesh, even if they are Christians by name, cannot truly know or please God.

The work of the Holy Spirit is discerned or sensed spiritually, and it is only by the Spirit that anyone can truly know God. We expect Christians to walk in the Spirit, but there are many self-proclaimed believers who still walk in the flesh, and from God's perspective, they are immature. These believers might be in Christ but are still like babies in their faith. Paul addresses them as such in 1 Corinthians 2:14-16 (NIV):

> *The person without the Spirit does not accept the things that come from the Spirit of God but considers them foolishness, and cannot understand them because they are discerned only through the Spirit. The person with the Spirit makes judgments about all things, but such a person is not subject to merely human judgments, for, "Who has known the mind of the Lord so as to instruct him?" But we have the mind of Christ.*

And 1 Corinthians 3:1-3 (NIV) states:

*Brothers and sisters, I could not address you as people who live by the Spirit but as people who are still worldly—mere infants in Christ. I gave you milk, not solid food, for you were not yet ready for it. Indeed, you are still not ready. You are still worldly. For since there is jealousy and quarreling among you, are you not worldly? Are you not acting like mere humans?*

Those who are immature or in the flesh are jealous and cause division and problems for the Church. They do not follow God but men and try to please and fear men—but our faith is in Jesus Christ alone, and we live to please Him. Romans 8:5-6 (NKJV) also makes the same distinction:

*For those who live according to the flesh set their minds on the things of the flesh, but those who live according to the Spirit, the things of the Spirit. For to be carnally minded is death, but to be spiritually minded is life and peace.*

Those who are truly in Christ Jesus do not feel judged by others nor do they feel the need to please people, though we honor all people. Instead, they experience continual peace, which is the natural fruit of living a Spirit-led life. No matter what trials, turbulence, or troubles come their way, they live in life and peace. Those who live according to the Spirit desire to please God and fulfill His will; and as a result, they have peace that transcends circumstances and naturally spread that peace to others around them. This kind of life is available to anyone who repents, surrenders their heart, mind, plans, and soul to Jesus Christ as their Lord and Savior!

## RECONCILIATION AND INTIMACY WITH GOD

At its core, the spiritual life is about reconciliation with God and then enjoying intimate fellowship with Him. Because God is with and within us, this peace flows into our relationships with others, even with our enemies. First Corinthians 3:2 illustrates the difference between baby and mature Christians, with milk representing the diet of new believers and solid food representing the deeper truths for those who have grown in their faith.

A key sign of immaturity is that these cause division and strife. Ego and self-centeredness are at the heart of the fleshly nature, which stands opposed to God. Only by the Spirit and the grace of Christ can we become less self-centered and more focused on living for God and others.

When we are born, we are naturally focused on our own ego, and all our judgments of right and wrong stem from self-interest. However, the danger in the faith journey is that believers can have both a spiritual and a carnal nature within them. In other words, even spiritual Christians can slip into carnality.

The key is that we still have two natures, and we need to guard our hearts for Jesus. Though we are born again, we are still capable of becoming carnal when we choose to let go of God and become self-centered. This is why Paul talks about the need for continual dependence on Jesus in Romans 7:24-25. We must deny ourselves daily, ask for His help, and live for Him every day. This is the true way of faith, and this is what Jesus means when He teaches His disciples to take up their cross and follow Him.

> *Then Jesus said to His disciples, "If anyone desires to come after Me, let him deny himself, and take up his cross, and follow Me. For whoever desires to save his life will lose it, but whoever loses his life for My sake will find it"* (Matthew 16:24-25 NKJV).

Though we may waver throughout the day between carnal and spiritual mindsets or natures, we must humbly acknowledge that this is the real us—*me*—with two natures, not someone else! There's no time for judging or trying to fix others when we ourselves are in need of God's help. Instead, we can humbly grow and sanctify one another by seeking God's help, growing in grace, and stopping the habit of judging others. It's so easy to focus on the "plank" in someone else's eye (Matthew 7:3-4), but the true challenge is for us to make a decision to grow in the grace and knowledge of Jesus Christ!

How can we continually abide in Jesus and strive for higher standards? When we pray, God takes over our hearts and minds. Our part is to pray, to consume the Word daily, and to acknowledge God moment by moment throughout the day. Romans 8:26 will begin to be a reality in our lives sooner than we expect.

## A LIFESTYLE OF PRAYER

Prayer does not have to be just a formal event; it is a lifestyle. We can pray with our eyes open, meaning we can engage in prayer while we're working, walking, and living life. Our hearts and minds can stay connected to God, whether we are in the Word, walking in the Spirit, or simply conversing with Him as we go about our day.

Jeremiah 23:23-24 reminds us that God is everywhere, and He sees all things. There is no place where we can escape from His presence, and He's constantly near us, ready to help. When we live with this constant awareness, prayer becomes a natural part of our everyday life, connecting us to His heart and allowing us to walk in His presence moment by moment.

> *"Am I a God near at hand," says the Lord, "And not a God afar off? Can anyone hide himself in secret places, so I shall not see him?" says the Lord; "Do I not fill heaven and earth?" says the Lord* (Jeremiah 23:23-24 NKJV).

How do we put to death the fleshly nature and live by the Spirit? Though there are billions of people here on earth, there are only three types of people in God's eyes. We must learn to stop judging and condemning ourselves and begin to see ourselves as God sees us. We must learn to see ourselves in Jesus Christ. Do not let any other, or even yourself, judge you. Rather, always see yourself in Jesus Christ, as the righteousness of God in you, and you will become healthy within, in heart and spirit. Some churches teach this topic under the word "Identity," or knowing oneself in Jesus Christ.

How can we love our neighbors as ourselves and love God with our all daily? We can show others love, mercy, and grace, as objects of mercy and love, when we ourselves learn how much God really loves us. Why does God command us to love Him with all our hearts, minds, souls, and strengths? This is because God loves us with all His heart, mind, soul, and strength! First John 4:10 (NKJV) tells us: *"In this is love, not that we loved God, but that He loved us and sent His Son to be the propitiation* [sacrifice] *for our sins."*

## OUR DUAL NATURE

God's love is not for someone else—it is for you. First Corinthians 2:14-16 speaks to this truth. The spiritual person is not judged by others, but is able to rightly judge all things because the mind of Christ is in a spiritual person. Romans 8:5-6 also clarifies that we have two natures, and we must learn to submit to Christ, even though we are weak as human beings.

Nevertheless, when our minds and hearts are set on Jesus, we can live, not die. We can go to Heaven and avoid hell. A Christian has two natures, and this remains true until the day we die, contrary to the idea of sinless perfection taught by Wesleyan holiness theology. We pray because we are weak. And when we pray that God Himself helps us to walk and live in the Spirit and continually have the mind of Christ (Matthew 26:41).

Galatians 5:16-18 shows us that we have two natures. Romans 8:12-14 also teaches about this dual nature; but through prayer, in Jesus, the Spirit, and the Word, we can have victory and not die spiritually. This is where free will, choice, and responsibility come into play. We can choose to be led by the Spirit, and there is space for spiritual discipline, which allows God's grace to increase in our lives. Romans 8:26-27 clarifies that we can become more spiritual and not live with one foot in the world and another in the church. We can choose to ask God for help. When we pray, the Spirit Himself intercedes for us because He knows the mind of Christ.

The flesh, or sinful nature, is ultimately self-centered. That old nature constantly tries to take center stage, putting ourselves in God's place to control everything (just look at the evil kings and rulers throughout history). The minute we let go and yield to our sinful nature, it can feel as if we never believed in God. This is the reality of sanctification, of spiritual growth, in any believer's life.

However by the Spirit, not by our own strength, we can become selfless, sacrificial, and see others as God sees them. The Holy Spirit can crucify our sinful nature and put it to death. Right now, we too can live and walk with Jesus, and have the mind of Christ. Who are you when no one is watching? God sees all, *El-Roi* is His name, and we must learn to crucify sin, grow in holiness, and please God by walking in the Spirit.

We have all been disappointed with ourselves at times, myself included. We compare ourselves to others who seem more spiritual and end up feeling sorry for ourselves, which can lead to frustration for those seeking to walk the Christian walk. What is the solution? Do not focus on yourself. *Fix your eyes on Jesus.* This is the essence of true biblical Christian faith.

Can we overcome the flesh? Yes we can—through Jesus Christ and the Holy Spirit. We must also focus on and imitate those who are loving others, building others up, and walking in the fruit of the Spirit. We must not focus on the fleshly or religious Christians (immature) who dishonor God's Son. Join a community of believers who are on fire for Jesus. Though no church is perfect, there are churches today filled with God's love and Spirit, with saints who are living according to God's Word. God will guide you. Simply ask Him for His help.

It is not always easy to pray, and some Christians don't pray. But when you see those who pray without wavering, you notice they are strong and mature in Christ because they've learned to let go of selfishness and the flesh. By faith, by trust in God's goodness, they pray daily, on their knees, building their lives, the Church, and the nations. As we do the same, God gives us dreams, encounters, visions, and even trances. The Holy Spirit truly prays for and through us. What a blessing and honor that is!

## FOCUS ON GOD'S WORD

I encourage you to memorize the following verses. When we meditate on and memorize the Bible, we become more and more like Jesus. Romans 8:26-27 (NKJV):

> *Likewise the Spirit also helps in our weaknesses. For we do not know what we should pray for as we ought, but the Spirit Himself makes intercession for us with groanings which cannot be uttered. Now He who searches the hearts knows what the mind of the Spirit is, because He makes intercession for the saints according to the will of God.*

Learn to memorize and pray the Scriptures. Do not get disappointed or offended at people. All people are prone to weakness, and God's grace is the only power that allows people to obey God. We are all sinful, weak, and need Jesus' grace. We also need to have healthy boundaries. We need to love other people, help people to become strong again in grace (called intercessory prayer), and to forgive the unforgivable, love the unlovable, and bless the unblessable.

Luke 6:28 (NKJV) is a command from God, not a suggestion: *"bless those who curse you, and pray for those who spitefully use you."*

The more we diligently train ourselves to memorize and meditate on God's Word, the easier it becomes to do so in the future. It is true. Life has its ups and downs, and we can go from feeling discouraged to encouraged, from high to low. Our hearts know both pain and joy.

However, we must pray to our Father in Heaven that our hearts grow strong and filled with God's presence, not weak and consumed by darkness. Our hearts go through seasons, from strength to weakness, but these are not really times of becoming stronger or weaker. They are simply cycles, and God knows everything we are going through.

What we can learn to do is cling to God in those moments, seek His grace, and ask for more consistency in our walk with Jesus every day. Only by His grace can we have true victory, and the more we focus on His Word and Spirit, the more our sinful nature is crucified by His grace.

## GOD'S GRACE

Many Christians and churches talk about "the grace of God," but what exactly is grace? Grace is love, love that is unconditional, undeserved, unfailing, and unexpected love.

Born-again Christians still struggle with two opposing natures; we need God's grace and His love to be victorious each day. We are weak, no one is perfect, not even in the church—no one except Jesus Christ. Regardless, it is our responsibility and within our free will to do so, to memorize and meditate on God's Word, to "put on" Christ, and have the mind of Christ, refusing to live in the flesh any longer.

Worries and anxieties come to both Christians and non-Christians alike. However we, as followers of Christ, have the ability to put on His mind and nature, to show mercy to others, and to not judge or hate, because hatred is of darkness. Proverbs 4:23 (NIV) tells us, *"Above all else, guard your heart, for everything you do flows from it."* It's so important to strengthen our hearts with God's grace (Hebrews 13:9).

In other words, we must open our hearts like little children, receiving God's love for us in Christ Jesus. For the Kingdom of God belongs to the childlike, not childish!

> *Then Jesus called a little child to Him, set him in the midst of them, and said, "Assuredly, I say to you, unless you are converted and become as little children, you will by no means enter the kingdom of heaven. Therefore whoever humbles himself as this little child is the greatest in the kingdom of heaven"* (Matthew 18:2-4 NKJV).

Please pray this prayer now: "Father God, I want to lay down my life and live for You and Your Kingdom. Take over all my heart, life, past, present, and future, I surrender all to You and Your Gospel purposes. Use me for the glory of Jesus and for Your glory, Lord!"

So what is grace? Grace is love! Grace and love are the same words; they are interchangeable. The only difference is that when we *receive* love, it is called grace. When we *give* love, it is called love! Grace is another way of saying "receiving love." There are two types of love—giving love, and receiving love.

Colossians 3:5-6 (NKJV) tells us: *"Therefore put to death your members which are on the earth: fornication, uncleanness, passion, evil desire, and covetousness, which is idolatry. Because of these things the wrath of God is coming upon the sons of disobedience."*

Also, Romans 8:14 (NIV) reveals to us this spiritual gold, *"For those who are led by the Spirit of God are the children of God."* Be led by the Spirit by receiving God's love, or grace. To summarize, there are three major types of love, or grace: Unexpected love, as seen in John 20:19-23 (NKJV)—the resurrected Jesus shows Himself to His disciples:

> *Then, the same day at evening, being the first day of the week, when the doors were shut where the disciples were assembled, for fear of the Jews, Jesus came and stood in the midst, and said to them, "Peace be with you." When He had said this, He showed them His hands and His side. Then the disciples were glad when they saw the Lord. So Jesus said to them again, "Peace to you! As the Father has sent Me, I also send you." And when He had said this, He breathed on them, and said to them, "Receive the Holy Spirit. If you forgive the sins of any, they are forgiven them; if you retain the sins of any, they are retained."*

## GOD'S LOVE

God reveals His Son to us in unexpected ways, just like He did to the disciples who were shocked by His resurrection. They thought Jesus was dead, but He came to them alive. This shows us that we don't seek God first—God seeks us out and comes to us. He loved us first! And He often comes to us at the most unexpected times. *"We love Him because He first loved us"* (1 John 4:19 NKJV).

We have received forgiveness from God, and because of that, we must forgive others. When we lack love, we won't reach out to the lost or the least, but when we have the love of Jesus in our hearts, when we have grace in our hearts, we will naturally go to those who need it the most. Grace is, at its core, unconditional love. God loves us with no strings attached. He is always faithful and always there for us.

Grace is also unchanging love. God's mercy is steadfast and unwavering. Unlike human love, which can be fickle and change, God's love remains the same, yesterday, today, and forever. Jesus' love for us never falters—it is fresh and new each and every morning.

In John 20:19-23, we see Jesus Christ speaking to His disciples after His resurrection. Death could not hold Him down, and He is no longer in the grave—as the result, you and I no longer have to fear death—we have assurance of salvation!

Did you know that the opposite of love is not hate but fear? "Do not fear" is written 365 times in the Bible. Every day we can trust and rely on our God who loves us and is with us.

Christianity is not just about receiving forgiveness; it is about living as those who have been forgiven, and part of that is forgiving others. The supernatural love and energy that come from God not only enable us to forgive, but also compel us to forgive and love first. This love extends to every area of our lives: at work, at home, with friends, family, and even strangers. We become God's unexpected agents of love, spreading His surprising love wherever we go.

God pours His love into our hearts through the Holy Spirit who dwells in anyone who repents and surrenders. When we surrender in prayer, not just to impose our own will but to fully receive His, we open ourselves to receive His love. During those moments, He fills us with His thoughts, His plans, His heart, His purpose. With that love, we can forgive the unforgivable, love the unlovable, and bless those we thought impossible to bless. Love never fails. It always overcomes, believes in others, hopes for others, bears with others, and endures through all things (1 Corinthians 13).

The love of God in Christ Jesus empowers us to overcome any and all circumstances, trials, and tests in life. Glory to God! When we surrender to His love, fear has no place in us. We are free to live in His *agape* love, never again living in fear, but always living in His perfect love. This is our privilege as children of God.

Any complaints or disappointments we may have with God or others fade away as we grow in His love. As 1 John 4:17-19 (NKJV) reminds us:

> *Love has been perfected among us in this: that we may have boldness in the day of judgment; because as He is, so are we in this world. There is no fear in love; but perfect* ***love casts out fear****, because fear involves torment. But he who fears has not been made perfect in love.* ***We love Him because He first loved us****.*

# 7

# SEEING HEAVEN BRIEFLY

In the summer of 1999, God allowed me to experience a glimpse of Heaven. But even after seeing hell, hearing the voice of Jesus, and receiving the baptism of the Holy Spirit, I found myself back in the world a few months later. How could this happen? The truth is, I was not discipled by anyone more spiritually mature at the time, and I had my own flawed understanding of Scripture. I wish now that I would have had someone to hold me accountable, someone to guide me through my journey of faith.

Back then, I remember reading somewhere in the Bible that God is merciful and forgiving, and those words really stuck with me. However, I did not fully grasp their meaning, especially since I had come from a background where forgiveness wasn't even a concept. In Buddhism, you have to pay for every sin through prayers and good deeds, whether in this life or the next, and no one knows how many lifetimes it might take. You are trapped in an endless cycle where your past sins dictate your current situation—whether you are rich or poor, it is all a result of what you've done in past lives. It feels like a never-ending, hopeless cycle, and it's hard to see any way out.

During that time, I did not know any better, and I believed whatever the monks taught me. But when I encountered the truth in the Bible about God's forgiveness, I thought, *Okay, God is good, and He forgives. I'm going to go to the nightclub one more time. Just one last time.* I convinced myself that it would not be the end of the world. I thought, *God is merciful, and I won't die just because I go back to this part of my old life one more time.* So I got in my car and drove to the club.

On the way back home, I was involved in a terrible car accident. I was driving my mom's Honda Accord while I was buzzed, and before I realized what happened, the car was on the curb and made an unexpected U-turn onto the freeway, facing the wrong direction. I was crossing over three lanes of traffic, and the tire blew out. Cars were honking at me, but somehow I managed to safely exit the freeway and pull over. Later, my mom told me she had been praying that night, asking God to send an angel to protect me because she felt something was wrong. Thank God for mothers who pray for their children.

## BALANCING ACT

During my first year as a Christian, I tried to balance my partying with my faith. I would tell people that God is merciful, but my actions were completely contradictory to what I was saying. I was not living a life that would draw anyone to Christ. One foot in the world and one foot in faith just does not work.

Another night, I was driving on the 5 South freeway, returning home from a club, when I hit a box in the middle of the road. From a distance, it looked like a brown paper shopping bag. However as I got closer, it turned out to be a huge crate box. My car, a new Acura Integra, was severely damaged. The police arrived, yelling at us to get out and find another way home. My car was towed away, and my friend and I were left shaken by the whole incident.

There was also a time when I crashed my car into a church wall while speeding on a local road. I thought the car was going to explode, so I jumped out through the window in panic. Moment after moment, God was trying to get my attention. Through each accident, He made it clear—my days of backsliding and partying were over. After three accidents, I finally got the message.

Out of the fear of the Lord, I stopped partying. It was not even out of an obedient or surrendered heart back then. It was just a selfish reason: I do not want to get hurt by God or get into another near-death car accident. As Saint Augustine, the famous early church father says in his classic book *The Confessions,* "I was a sinner lost but trying to come back." (This work highlights his personal journey of deep struggle with sin before finding redemption and conversion to Christianity, openly confessing his past failings while praising God's grace that allowed him to find his way back to the faith.)

I still felt traumatized by my visit to hell, but my sinful nature still wanted to come out and fulfill its cravings. I finally prayed, "O God, I need Your help. I need grace from You." And in June 1999, the Lord God Almighty, in His goodness and mercy, allowed me a brief visit to Heaven.

This experience happened right in the midst of my partying days—talk about God's perfect timing and grace. Hallelujah! While we were still sinners, Christ died for you and me.

In this dream, I vividly remember my family and I living through the Great Tribulation, the end times on earth. Christians were being arrested, martyred, and executed. Government agents were chasing us, but by God's grace, we somehow managed to escape. We kept driving, eventually reaching the top of a very high mountain. While standing on the top of the mountain peak, I saw the most beautiful and vast green valley, with a beautiful river flowing through the middle.

My family and I stood there, victorious, covered by the blood of the Lamb. We were standing on that mountain, gazing out over the lush valley. Then I looked up and the heavens opened, and I saw the New Jerusalem descending from Heaven. The city was clothed in transparent gold, shining magnificently. It was unlike anything I had ever seen, brilliant and beautiful, glowing with divine light. As I looked on, I could hear the voices of countless angels, praising and worshiping God. Their voices were so pure, so heavenly, and I knew without a doubt that this wasn't the voice of human beings. I wondered to myself, *How could created beings sing so beautifully?* I just knew in my spirit that it was the heavenly chorus of angels.

The words from Revelation 21:2 (NIV) came to my mind: *"And I saw the Holy City, the new Jerusalem, coming down out of heaven from God, prepared as a bride beautifully dressed for her husband."*

Then, God appeared to me as a brilliant, glorious ball of light that shifted into a triangle of pure radiance. I believe this is how God might have appeared to the apostle Paul during his conversion experience. And when God came, it was not for small talk. He did not ask me if I liked extra pepperoni on my pizza. He came with words from His Word. He said, *"Jesus is My beloved Son, in whom I am well pleased. Listen to Him. Listen to Him. Listen to Him."*

I did not fully realize it at the time, but later I discovered those exact words are repeated in three of the four Gospels. God repeated them to me three times, His voice ringing in my heart, confirming His truth.

> *While he was still speaking, behold, a bright cloud overshadowed them; and suddenly a voice came out of the cloud, saying, "This is My beloved Son, in whom I am well pleased. Hear Him!"* (Matthew 17:5 NKJV)

In the dream, when I heard that voice, I said to myself, *Oh my gosh! I heard the voice of the Son before, but this is the voice of the Father God!* And then I woke up from my dream. I was in awe and wonder as I shared with my family during that day's breakfast table that I had just heard the heavenly Father's voice, testifying of how pleased He is with His Son Jesus. I shared how we must listen to Him. They replied, "You are right, Steve, it is time for you to listen to Jesus and obey, not just talk about faith, but live it out and show us." And that was my exit out of the party scene.

# 8

# ONLY THE BLOOD OF JESUS SAVES HUMANITY FROM HELL

When our hearts and consciences are washed by the blood of Jesus, that is when we can truly begin to hear the voice of God. The blood of Jesus made a way for humanity to have restored fellowship and intimacy with God, as if we had never sinned. That is the Good News.

In John 10:27 (NKJV), Jesus Himself says, *"My sheep hear My voice, and I know them, and they follow Me."* After I repented for not listening to Jesus, I began to hear His voice more clearly in my heart, the still, small voice in my spirit. My mind was filled more and more with His Word.

There is a powerful story from the days of Japanese imperialistic occupation of South Korea. A student rose up and sparked a revolution, and it was not a hidden event. Most Koreans know about it to this day. Students flooded the streets, shouting *"Mansei!"* ("Hooray!"). That is when Japanese soldiers, on horseback, charged in with long sticks and began beating the students. At first, they did not use machine guns; they struck the students with sticks. However to their surprise, the students did not scatter or run. Instead, the students who were struck were marked with stick marks on their bodies. These marks were a sign, a way for the soldiers to later identify them, in order to arrest them.

## THE BLOOD OF THE LAMB

Now here is the powerful truth. As those students were marked by their wounds, the Israelites were also marked, but by God Himself. They were set apart, sealed by God's own mark for a divine purpose.

> *Now the blood shall be a sign for you on the houses where you are. And when I see the blood, I will pass over you; and the plague shall not be on you to destroy you when I strike the land of Egypt* (Exodus 12:13 NKJV).

In the book of Exodus, we see that God Himself desired to rescue His people Israel, and therefore commanded Moses to mark His people with blood. Let's now carefully examine and consider what the Bible says regarding blood, before and after this historical event of blood deliverance called the Passover.

> *...On the tenth day of this month every man shall take for himself a lamb, according to the house of his father, a lamb for a household* (Exodus 12:3 NKJV).

The lamb had to be a year old and completely spotless. A year-old lamb is at its prime health, and for the Passover it also had to be the best quality. One that was neither wild nor tainted. This Passover lamb symbolizes the Lamb of God who was to carry the sins of the world, Jesus Christ.

The Lamb of God prepared before the foundation of the world to carry the sins of the world is pure and humble; and if we will learn from Him, we too will have true peace and rest. This is how the pure, year-old lamb represents Christ Jesus. God sent the Israelites to Egypt that they might be tested, and then He rescued them thru the Passover lamb that each family sacrificed. This act foreshadowed the Lamb of God who was to come about 1,400 years later to bear the sins of the world.

The Israelites were instructed to kill the lamb and *"take some of the blood and put it on the two doorposts and on the lintel of the houses where they eat it"* (Exodus 12:6-7 NKJV). The lamb had to shed its blood—it was destined to die. This pure, spotless lamb was chosen to die for God's chosen people.

It is not wrong to say that even before the sacrificial system was fully established through Moses and the Levitical priesthood, this was an early form of Israel's sacrificial system. The people who ate the lamb had to apply its blood to their doorposts, and those who didn't partake of the lamb couldn't use its blood to escape the angel of death.

Those who ate the lamb were the elect of Israel. Similarly, only those who partake of the Lamb of God, Jesus, who takes away the sins of the world, can apply His blood to themselves. As Jesus says, *"This is My body which is given for you"* (Luke 22:19 NKJV). Those who eat the flesh of Jesus receive the mark of His blood.

God instructed through Moses that the lamb must be roasted in the fire. This foreshadows Christ's own suffering on the Cross. Eating the unleavened bread quickly represents holiness, and the urgency to leave Egypt symbolizes the need to repent immediately (Exodus 34:25; Deuteronomy 16:3). The bitter herbs remind us of the oppression Israel faced in Egypt and the oppression we face in the world system (Exodus 1:14).

Interestingly, any leftovers of the lamb had to be burned in the fire. This command helps prevent people from idolizing the lamb itself or returning to Egypt. We humans are prone to superstition, and if we don't guard our hearts, we can start worshiping objects instead of the living God. This is why God commanded the Israelites to burn the leftovers.

> *And thus you shall eat it: with a belt on your waist, your sandals on your feet, and your staff in your hand. So you shall eat it in haste. It is the Lord's Passover* (Exodus 12:11 NKJV).

The attire of the Israelites during Passover mirrored the dress of pilgrims. They were leaving Egypt, fully prepared for a long journey ahead. In the same way, we too must remember that we are aliens and strangers here on earth, on a journey to our true home—Heaven.

Peter reminds us, *"Beloved, I beg you as sojourners and pilgrims, abstain from fleshly lusts which war against the soul"* (1 Peter 2:11 NKJV). Jesus calls us pilgrims, reminding us that our home is not here, but in Heaven. When we forget we're pilgrims, we begin to attach ourselves to the fleeting pleasures of the world. We forget that our true home is Heaven and grieve God by allowing sin to take root in our lives.

This is also why Communion is so important. It's a reminder that, like the Israelites in Egypt, we are on a pilgrimage. Every time we take Communion, we should remember that we are on a journey to our heavenly home. It's not just about partaking in the elements—it's about living out that pilgrimage lifestyle in faith, with our hearts and minds set on our true destination.

The Israelites were commanded to "gird their waist with truth" (Ephesians 6:14), which speaks to the need for strength, integrity, and discernment. We must walk through life with a firm commitment to what is true. In a world that constantly tells us to bend or blur moral lines, we must stand firm in the truth of God's Word. Living with integrity means choosing what is right, even when it's not the popular or easy thing to do.

To lose sight of truth and no longer be able to discern what is right or wrong shows that we've lost our foundation. In today's world, post-modernism, moral relativism, and political correctness all encourage us to ignore clear distinctions between right and wrong. But to truly live means to know who we are in Christ, to be honest with ourselves, and to depend fully on Jesus. The person who truly believes in Jesus is the one who acknowledges their faults and sins, rather than focus on the faults of others.

Those of us on this pilgrimage must "know ourselves." We must acknowledge our weaknesses and realize that we cannot move forward without Jesus' help. He is the One who helps us persevere through the storms of life. It's only through Him that we can walk this journey with strength, resolve, and faith.

## WITH SANDALS ON YOUR FEET

It is comfortable to walk with shoes or sandals that fit well. Walking with shoes that do not fit or are worn out is painful and slows down the journey. Those who are about to run a marathon are dressed lightly, and not only are their sneakers light, but their strings are tied tightly for the race ahead.

As pilgrims, what kind of sandals or shoes are we to walk with? Ephesians states that we are to put on the *"shoes of the Gospel of peace."* The Gospel itself is given by our Lord, the Provider, and is not created by man or in a factory. The Gospel is from God Himself, and it is a gift from Him to you. We are to simply receive it, by faith.

Isaac simply received his inheritance from his father, Abraham. There was nothing he did with his own stressful effort. Yes, that is correct. And this is the essence of the Gospel. When we were sinners, Jesus Christ died in our place, and He rose from the dead to give us new life and to restore our place as His children. Jesus ascended on high to sit at the right hand of the Father, and even desires to give us the same glory that He has.

These are the most important themes of the Gospel. And there is nothing found that we accomplished. Everything has been and is prepared by God Himself, and we must believe that our job is to simply receive. Our part is to simply believe that God has prepared all things and we are to put on the shoes of the Gospel of peace and walk toward

Heaven as pilgrims and sojourners. However, from time to time, we try to put on the shoes we made for ourselves. When we put on these different shoes, we either head toward the wrong direction or fall and injure ourselves.

## WITH YOUR STAFF IN YOUR HAND

A staff is something the traveler can lean on. In the same way, we who are walking toward Heaven as pilgrims can lean on the staff of faith. As a matter of fact, without faith we cannot leave or start the journey. We do not know how long the journey will be, and where to rest during the journey, and how to face hunger. Are there really reliable plans as we walk even with the elderly and our flock? Of course there are neither plans nor calculations that will work, only faith. We must simply leave Egypt. We must walk toward Canaan without hesitation, for God has granted it to us—but how can we if we do not have faith?

## EAT HASTILY

There's no time for hesitation. If Pharaoh's heart softens, we might end up staying in Egypt. Just like the Israelites had to leave as a united community, no one could afford to hesitate or change their mind. God rescued Lot's wife, but she was destroyed because she looked back. Jesus warns that *"No one who puts a hand to the plow and looks back is fit for service in the kingdom of God"* (Luke 9:62 NIV).

The fire is raging, and there's no time to linger. We need to act decisively and quickly, snatching others from the fire. If we hesitate or wait too long, the tempter and devourer will attack.

## JUDGMENT

> *On that same night I will pass through Egypt and strike down every firstborn of both people and animals, and I will bring judgment on all the gods of Egypt. I am the Lord* (Exodus 12:12 NIV).

Judgment is inevitable. Where will it take place? In Egypt! God's judgment falls on Egypt, the land that oppressed His people. Those who exploit others for their own gain, who trample over them without mercy, will not go unpunished. Without justice, the oppressed would have no hope. But our God is the God of justice. "I am God," and that alone is enough.

The oppressors will not have the power to oppress forever. The oppressed will not suffer forever. The day will come when God will bring judgment. *"On that same night,"* the night God chooses, He will move through Egypt, the land that killed, oppressed, and squeezed the life out of God's chosen people. And this judgment will cover the whole land—not just a small part, but all of it.

God judges all—just as He sends rain to both the righteous and the unrighteous, His judgment touches everyone. There's no one who can escape on their own merit. There's no point in crying out that it's unfair. *"Vengeance is Mine,"* says the Lord in Romans 12:19 (NKJV). He sees everything, and He knows everything. Therefore, we must live righteous lives. Even when we're oppressed, angry, or victimized, we must trust in the Lord to carry out His judgment. It's foolish to think we must take matters into our own hands, as if God doesn't see or doesn't know.

It's also unwise to think that just because God doesn't judge immediately, He has forgotten. We live in a world full of people who have no fear of God's judgment, and many atheists who believe life just goes on without Him. But they can't delay death for even a moment. People who ignore God's judgment without fear are heading for destruction. *"In the past God overlooked such ignorance, but now he commands all people everywhere to repent"* (Acts 17:30 NIV). In the past, God might have been patient, but now, with so much revelation and understanding of God's existence, the call for repentance is urgent. Without repentance, judgment will be even more dreadful.

This isn't just someone else's issue—it's mine, too. I must examine myself. Are there areas of my life that might fall under judgment? The Lord who passed through the land of Egypt is searching our hearts and lives, too. Am I only focused on moral living? Am I using my faith for personal gain? Even if I know biblical truths, does my life reflect them? If I have the Gospel, do I share it with others, or am I stubbornly hoarding it for myself?

God's justice is complete, righteous, and thorough. His judgment falls on people, animals, and even the false gods that people worship. His justice is total—it covers everything. If the eye sins, it will be plucked out; if the hand sins, it will be cut off. We cannot escape the judgment of a righteous God. No matter the situation or circumstance, judgment will always be complete and thorough.

The reality of judgment brings order, and when judgment is ignored, chaos prevails. In a society where order is often dismissed or even dismantled, governments at all levels have to step in and restore order through judgment. This principle is taught in Scripture and echoed throughout history.

It's hard to claim that our culture is without disorder, especially in today's world. It's no different from the time of the judges in Israel, when *"everyone did as they saw fit"* (Judges 21:25 NIV). When there's no order, society falls apart. I'm concerned that judgment might first come upon believers if we continue living according to our own opinions and desires. If we live according to what seems right to us, we are only deceiving ourselves and inviting judgment.

There's no escaping judgment when we base our lives solely on our own opinions. Simply listening to a sermon about how God judged Egypt while remaining ignorant of our own impending judgment is foolish. It's like a blind man leading another blind man. Just as Egypt faced judgment for oppressing God's people, so will anyone who refuses to acknowledge Christ as the Head of the Church, who ignores His will and stubbornly lives according to their own.

## THE BLOOD GOSPEL

It's surprising that Egypt was judged through God's ten plagues, but even more surprising is the fact that some homes were spared during that judgment. This is where we find the Gospel—the Blood Gospel.

> *The blood will be a sign for you on the houses where you are; and when I see the blood, I will pass over you. No destructive plague will touch you when I strike Egypt* (Exodus 12:13 NIV).

Even though judgment came upon Egypt, homes marked with blood were spared. This is God's mercy—a mercy we should be incredibly grateful for. This method was not man-made; it was revealed by God Himself. He commanded the Israelites to sacrifice a lamb and apply its blood to the doorposts. This act displayed the fear of the Lord's judgment and obedience to His Word.

Many say they fear God's judgment, but they don't obey Him. Though they claim to fear the Lord's judgment, they live however they please, trying to avoid judgment by their own effort. If we truly fear God's judgment, we must obey His Word. Obedience according to God's commands solves all problems. The lamb was sinless, yet it was judged and shed its blood.

When the blood is applied to the doorposts, it exempts us from judgment. This is the Gospel—the Blood Gospel.

> *Behold! The Lamb of God who takes away the sin of the world!* (John 1:29 NKJV)

The lambs God instructed the Israelites to sacrifice in Egypt were a foreshadowing of *"the Lamb of God."* We couldn't approach God on our own, so He became a man and dwelt among us—His name is Jesus (John 1:14). Jesus is God's Lamb. He died in our place, hung on a tree, took our judgment, and anyone who believes in His blood is forgiven, escapes judgment, and becomes a child of God. We can boldly cry out, "Abba, Father!" to God Himself.

Applying the blood of Christ to my heart is the essence of the Blood Gospel. Marking my life with His blood is the way to life, the only way to escape God's judgment. There is no other way to avoid judgment. That's why we sing, "Nothing but the blood of Jesus." Some say, "Just as Jesus sacrificed Himself, let us sacrifice ourselves for others." While this sounds noble, it can miss the core of the Blood Gospel. The Gospel isn't about becoming more altruistic or living a better life—it's about living under the blood to escape judgment.

To view Jesus' sacrifice simply as a moral standard or lifestyle is to trample on His blood. It's essentially cursing the blood of Jesus. You and I are not living sacrificially like Christ did. We are simply escaping judgment by being covered under His blood. It's dangerous to talk about living sacrificially when we are looking at the blood. When we lose sight of the atonement of Christ, we are deceived.

To have Christian faith means to live under the covering of the blood—not just to have a blood-spilling mindset, but to live with the blood applied to our hearts. If God sees the blood on us, that's all that matters.

"When I see the blood," we sing in hymns, and God does indeed see the blood! He doesn't see my passion or my abilities. He doesn't see my weaknesses or my good works. He simply sees the blood, and through it, I am saved. If we add up all our good works but don't have the blood, God will ignore them.

No matter what we might lack, when God sees the blood, we are delivered from judgment. This is what it means to have faith. This is the heart of Christianity. This is the Blood Gospel.

Does God see the blood on you? Have you applied the blood that God requires to forego judgment? There's nothing more tragic than a believer who doesn't have the blood. No matter how much passion or work we put into it, if the blood isn't there, it's not the faith God requires.

*"But now that you have come to know God, rather to be known by God"* (Galatians 4:9 ESV), we are to have faith that is acknowledged by God. He does not see outside of the blood. That is because nobody can appear before God without the blood in the first place. The blood has the power to cover all sin and to destroy all sin (Isaiah 1:18).

So, have you applied the blood for yourself? How does one apply the blood?

> *Here is a trustworthy saying that deserves full acceptance: Christ Jesus came into the world to save sinners—of whom I am the worst* (1 Timothy 1:15 NIV).

This Scripture shows us how to apply the blood to ourselves. Jesus came to shed His blood for sinners, and no matter how much we've sinned, we need His blood. It's not an exaggeration to say that the blood is ready to cleanse us the moment we sin. The blood doesn't just help us escape judgment; it also shields us from the consequences of sin's curses.

In the Old Testament, the blood also symbolizes a city of refuge—a complete covering, offering protection and safety. To live under the blood is to publicly proclaim our faith, and this is the core of Christianity—the Blood Gospel.

# 9

# MARKED BY THE BLOOD

**SO THIS DAY SHALL BE TO YOU A MEMORIAL; AND YOU SHALL KEEP IT AS A FEAST TO THE LORD THROUGHOUT YOUR GENERATIONS. YOU SHALL KEEP IT AS A FEAST BY AN EVERLASTING ORDINANCE (EXODUS 12:14 NKJV).**

Living under the blood of Christ is not a one-time thing; it's a daily reality. We're not called to apply the blood once and move on—it's something we need to celebrate and live under constantly. God commands us to make this a permanent, everlasting ordinance because it's not just about an event in the past; it's about continually abiding in His protection and grace. As long as we're here on earth, living in our earthly bodies, we'll inevitably get stained by the world around us. That's why we must return to the blood regularly, even though Jesus has already made us clean.

This isn't just for us—it's for every generation. God wants each one to see and experience the power of the blood, because we all need it. It would be heartbreaking for me to be covered by the blood but for my children or descendants to ignore it. Paul felt this burden for others too. In Romans 9:3 (NIV), he says, *"I could wish that I myself were cursed and cut off from Christ for the sake of my people, those of my own race,"* showing his heart for his people's salvation.

If we have a heart like Paul, we'll want to bring our whole family and loved ones under the blood of Jesus. It's hard to truly believe someone is living under the blood if they don't care about their family and others being covered by it too. Of course, we can't force anyone to accept it—that's something only God can do. But like Paul, we can pray. As he says in Romans 10:1 (NIV), *"Brothers and sisters, my heart's desire and prayer to God for the Israelites is that they may be saved."* We should pray for the salvation of those around us, that they too can live under the blood and experience God's grace and protection.

When we live under the blood, there's no way judgment can touch us. It's the safest place we can be—from judgment, from sin's curse, and from anything that could harm us. The blood is our ultimate refuge—both in this life and in the next. But it's not a one-time covering. It's something we need to continually return to, for ourselves and for the ones we love.

## THE CALLING

The calling of the priests to serve God is incredibly holy, and to set them apart for their duties, many ceremonies and regulations were necessary (Exodus 29:10-25). But if these acts were only about going through the motions, they wouldn't hold much meaning. Aaron's garments—the undergarments, ephod, robe, breastplate, belt, crown, and cords—weren't just beautiful; each piece had deep significance, given by God to remind the priest of his holy calling.

The priestly garments were designed with meaning in mind. If they're only worn to look impressive or to assert authority, they're just empty symbols—nothing more than dead skin. And if that attitude persists, all that will come of it is hypocrisy.

God's commands to Moses for Aaron and his sons to carry out their priestly duties and maintain the temple aren't just for them. They apply to us today as well. So, what role does the blood play in the priestly calling? Even though we're not Israelites or Levites, we've been given salvation through Jesus' blood and have become a nation of priests. Through His sacrifice, we now have access not just to the Holy Place but to the Most Holy Place at any time, as priests of the Most High God.

This holy calling is ours in this era of grace. As believers, we must never forget that, as priests, we too must apply the blood to ourselves. It's not just a historical practice—it's something that still matters today in our walk with God.

## THE BLOOD OF JESUS REDEEMS

When people brought the calf to the door of the tabernacle, Aaron and his sons had to lay their hands on its head (Exodus 29:10). This act symbolized the transfer of their sins to the animal. The priest's primary duty was to address the issue of sin, and the laying on of hands was how the sin was symbolically passed onto the calf. After that, Aaron and his sons had to catch the calf and kill it because it now had to shed its blood.

That blood represented redeeming blood and pointed forward to the blood of Jesus. Moses took his fingers, applied the calf's blood to the horns of the altar, and poured the rest out at the base (Exodus 29:12). The wages of sin, then as now, was death. The calf, carrying the sins of the people, had to die, and its blood had to be applied to the altar's horns, which symbolize the Cross.

The Lamb of God, Jesus, shed His blood on the Cross, marking the fulfillment of God's plan of redemption. This is what the Blood Gospel is all about—only blood can bring redemption. Throughout history, people have sought different ways to receive forgiveness for their sins. Some have gone on pilgrimages, lived ascetically in mountains, inflicted pain on themselves, fasted, or followed other religious practices. While some of these practices might have benefits, they are foolish attempts to deal with sin.

This confusion is not limited to outside the Christian faith. Even within Christianity, where we believe Jesus is the only Savior, people sometimes try to earn salvation through suffering or spiritual disciplines. But doing so is essentially rejecting the power of Jesus' blood and trampling on it. Yes, like Paul, we are called to discipline our bodies, as he says in 1 Corinthians 9:27 (NKJV), *"I discipline my body and bring it into subjection,"* but we must never confuse such practices with a requirement for salvation. That's a serious mistake.

We can see people trying to enter the Kingdom of Heaven without fully understanding Jesus' redemptive work. Some try to deal with sin on their own, others try to earn mercy through good works or buy papers that guarantee forgiveness. The world has always had these misconceptions. If we're not careful, we too can start mixing man-made efforts or righteousness with the grace of God, which is the essence of the Gospel. We must always be vigilant against this.

The principle of "life giving life" is why blood had to be shed—it's God's will. He prepared Christ as the sin offering, the ultimate example of this principle. All the protocols for sacrifice were given to Moses, and offerings to God must be done according to His Word. The way we serve God doesn't come from within us; it comes from God. Just because something seems right to us doesn't mean it's the right way to serve Him.

We simply obey as He has commanded us. The Blood Gospel is from God, and there is no remission of sins without His blood. And for the one who dies without remission of sin, there is judgment of hell awaiting.

Adonijah, Solomon's older brother, tried to exalt himself as king without King David's approval. He sacrificed lambs and gathered Joab, the commander, and Abiathar, the priest, to support him. But Nathan the prophet rebuked him, and Solomon was made king in his place. The noise in Jerusalem was so intense that it caused the earth to shake (1 Kings 1:40). Fearful of the chaos, Adonijah fled and took refuge in the house of God, grabbing hold of the horns of the altar (1 Kings 1:50).

The way to salvation was for Adonijah to recognize his sin and cling to the altar's horns. In the same way, as believers redeemed by the blood of Jesus, we too must hold tightly to the Cross, just as Adonijah did the horns. The blood has already been poured out beneath the altar, and this is where the truth of the Blood Gospel lies. It's through the blood of Christ that we find redemption, and we must continually cling to it.

The blood's effect is to forgive sin, for sin brings people to hell, but those under Jesus' blood escape the judgment of hell.

All of the lamb's blood was poured out beneath the altar. And before the Feast of Passover, knowing that His hour had come to leave this world and go to the Father, Jesus, having loved His own who were in the world, loved them to the very end (John 13:1). In other words, when Jesus loves us, He holds nothing back. His love is complete, all-consuming, and without reserve.

The blood Jesus shed on the Cross wasn't just part of His blood—it was all of it. And that's why we too are called to love Him with all our heart, mind, and strength. If we hold back any part of our love or devotion to God, something is missing. We must remember that all of His blood was poured out beneath the altar for our sins. This redemption is priceless, and we can never forget that Jesus gave everything for us.

We're not receiving just a partial redemption; all of His blood was shed for our redemption—every drop of it. As priests who serve the Lord, we must first recognize that we need that blood for ourselves. The priests of the Old Testament didn't just pour out the blood beneath the altar, they also applied it to their thumb and the horns of the altar. This points to the ministry of the Lamb of God, who would take up the Cross as the High Priest.

As priests of God today, it's a grave mistake to think of the Cross as simply a symbol of glory, as many in the world do. A cross without the blood isn't the Cross of Jesus. A cross that represents only success and glory is nothing more than vanity. We need to be careful not to defame the Cross by misrepresenting it. A cross without blood is a useless cross. In fact, it's not the cross Jesus asked us to bear daily, and we must repent if we're carrying a cross that doesn't reflect His sacrifice.

It is heartbreaking to see people carrying the cross to pursue their fleshly desires—whether for fame, success, or their own glory. The true Cross, the one we should be proud of, is the one stained with blood. As Paul says, *"the world has been crucified to me, and I to the world"* (Galatians 6:14 NKJV). This is the Cross we should embrace—the one that speaks of suffering, sacrifice, and the blood of Jesus.

While it's encouraging to see the symbol of the cross spread throughout the world, a cross that seeks only glory without understanding its true meaning—suffering, sacrifice, and bloodshed—is to ignore what the Cross really represents. Without the blood, the Cross becomes a hollow symbol of hypocrisy when people seek glory through it.

Carrying the Cross with the right heart means engaging in deep, sacrificial service—praying with labor, evangelizing with passion, serving God wholeheartedly in secret, and living to please Him. It's not just about recognizing the symbol of the cross, but about walking in the will of God by taking up our cross daily. This is the heart of our Father's desire for us.

## THE BLOOD OF SACRIFICE

Now more about the blood of the sacrifice.

This time, Aaron and his sons took a ram and offered it as a sin offering by laying their hands on it again (Exodus 29:15). This act symbolized the ram taking the place of the sinner. The ram, shedding its blood, was doing so on behalf of another. To place it on the altar was to offer it to God as a set-apart sacrifice. The blood wasn't something that could just be sprinkled and forgotten. All of it had to be given to God. And so, this redeemed life—our life—must be given in its entirety to Him.

Paul writes, *"I face death every day—yes, just as surely as I boast about you in Christ Jesus our Lord"* (1 Corinthians 15:31 NIV). Paul's life was daily sprinkled on the altar, just as Jesus shed all of His blood for us. We too must give every drop of our lives for Him. We can't sprinkle our blood anywhere else. It must be poured out only on the altar. This is a responsibility and a duty for all who know Him. But we must be careful—today, it seems like people are often praised for shedding their blood for Jesus, and receiving people's applause can rob us of the rewards God has for us in Heaven.

It is easy to fall into the trap of seeking recognition, and even martyrdom can be twisted into a desire for self-glory. Not all of us will be called to physical martyrdom, but true faith is about living as if we're already laying down our lives every day. It's not about waiting for the moment we're called to die for Him—it's about being ready to surrender everything at any time. This is what it means to *die daily,* and it reflects a life of daily sprinkling the blood on the altar.

We all sweat in our labor. And there is a sweetness that comes after hard work, but there are also things we can't accomplish no matter how hard we try. In those moments, people may turn to superstition or seek other sources of help, but we have the privilege of praying to the God for whom nothing is impossible.

There is a prayer of humility—a prayer with tears. It's the kind of prayer where we cry out, "God, I can't do this." It's a devotion expressed through tears. For those who have set themselves apart for God, there are levels of offering: First, we give all our strength and sweat to Him. Then, we offer our tears. Finally, we offer up our blood and our lives.

If we cannot live with just our sweat, we can offer our tears. If we can't offer our tears, we will struggle to offer our blood. Though these levels may not always happen in order, we must be ready to offer even our blood when the time comes.

Though we may not literally shed our blood every day, the attitude of self-sacrifice is what matters. As Paul says, *"I have fought the good fight, I have finished the race, I have kept the faith"* (2 Timothy 4:7). Those who keep the faith until the end are already martyrs in God's eyes, even if they never physically shed their blood. If you've kept the faith and given your all, your blood is already on God's altar.

Those whose names are written in the Book of Life are those who have shed their blood on the altar—whether through literal martyrdom or by living out devotion in every part of their lives. True faith means surrendering everything, and those who haven't given their blood to the altar cannot claim to have real faith.

The sacrificial system in the Old Testament required not just the sprinkling of blood but the slaughter of the animal, and all of its parts—its insides, legs, and head—were washed and burned on the altar (Exodus 29:17-18). Simply sprinkling the blood wasn't enough. The animal had to be completely offered, all of it, as a sacrifice to God.

## OFFERING ALL TO HIM

In the same way, we must offer all of ourselves to God. Our hands, feet, eyes, lips—all of it belongs to Him. But we don't just give parts of ourselves; we must give our whole bodies to God, just as He has washed us clean with His blood. The true sacrifice is a whole life laid down on the altar, burning in the fire of devotion.

At times, we may give Him our lips but not our hands or feet. Or we may offer ourselves without fully surrendering to His will. But if we don't fully offer ourselves—if we don't allow the fire to consume us completely—then it's not a pleasing aroma to God. We can't offer unclean sacrifices or ignore the sin offering God requires of us. We must obey God in how we offer our lives to Him.

Sacrifices can be both external and internal. While not all of us will be called to physically shed our blood on the altar, those who have kept the faith until the end have already made that sacrifice. Biblical faith is about surrendering our lives—our blood—for the Lord. It's not about whether we physically die for Him, it's about living our lives as though we've already died.

There is always temptation to deny Jesus, as Peter did. But even if we fail in one moment, the true test of faith is in how we live—are we willing to lay down our lives, even in the smallest ways, every day? The Lord sees our hearts. He knows when we are truly surrendered to Him.

> *Do not present your members as instruments of unrighteousness to sin, but present yourselves to God as being alive from the dead, and your members as instruments of righteousness to God* (Romans 6:13 NKJV).

Our bodies are temples of the Holy Spirit, bought at a price. We must glorify God in our bodies, living fully surrendered lives (1 Corinthians 6:19-20). The sacrifice He desires is not just in external acts, but in our whole lives, with our hearts laid down for His glory. That is a sure way to secure Heaven and avoid hell. Though we are saved by grace not works, such works prove that we have received real grace!

What is it about the blood that sanctifies us to live such saved, Heaven-assuring lives?

> *You shall also take the other ram, and Aaron and his sons shall put their hands on the head of the ram. Then you shall kill the ram, and take some of its blood and put it on the tip of the right ear*

> *of Aaron and on the tip of the right ear of his sons, on the thumb of their right hand and on the big toe of their right foot, and sprinkle the blood all around on the altar. And you shall take some of the blood that is on the altar, and some of the anointing oil, and sprinkle it on Aaron and on his garments, on his sons and on the garments of his sons with him; and he and his garments shall be hallowed, and his sons and his sons' garments with him* (Exodus 29:19-21 NKJV).

The priest would first sprinkle the blood that removes sin on the altar's horns, then the blood that gives life on the altar, and finally the blood that sanctifies at the end. This is why three animals were prepared. The lamb that sanctifies only shed its blood after Aaron and his sons laid their hands on its head, transferring the sins onto the lamb before it died.

## FIRST, MAKE YOUR EARS HOLY.

The lamb's blood was sprinkled on the right ears of Aaron and his sons. The ears are for hearing, and their sanctification represents our obedience to hearing God's Word. We must first be set apart in order to truly obey Him. As Samuel says, *"Has the Lord as great delight in burnt offerings and sacrifices, as in obeying the voice of the Lord? Behold, to obey is better than sacrifice"* (1 Samuel 15:22 NKJV).

The winds and waves obey God's Word, but humans—created in His image—often fail to obey. The Israelites were disciplined repeatedly for their disobedience, which is why it was essential that their ears were sanctified by the blood. Without this, they were unable to hear God's Word.

When we come to the Lord's altar to hear His Word, it cannot become revelation in our hearts unless our ears are cleansed by the blood. Some may have "lofty ears," meaning they only seek pleasant words or intellectual teachings, but this is not true spiritual hearing. Only ears washed in the blood can truly hear the revelation of God's Word.

This is why it's urgent for believers to have their ears sprinkled with the blood of Jesus. Many people go from church to church, chasing the latest sermon or emotional satisfaction, but remain spiritually shallow. The blood applied to our ears helps us hear and embrace the true depth of God's Word.

## MAKE YOUR HANDS HOLY.

The hands represent our work. Not working is a problem, but working without having the blood applied to our hands makes our efforts unacceptable to God. If we work merely for our own satisfaction and glory, our work is vanity, not worship.

Before we engage in any work, we need to examine whether the blood is sprinkled on our hands. Jesus' blood on our hands means we work not for ourselves but for His glory. The phrase "the blessing by the hands with the blood" speaks to the blessing that removes sin, reminding us that our hands—washed by His blood—should now be used to serve Him.

We must work for Jesus, with His blood on our hands, and with pure motives, rather than seeking personal recognition. When we do this, we can truly live out the principle that our left hand should not know what our right hand is doing (Matthew 6:3).

## MAKE YOUR FEET HOLY.

Our feet symbolize our actions—our deeds of faith. While salvation is through faith and not works, those saved by faith must still have their feet washed in the blood. Deeds without the blood of Jesus are man-centered and hypocritical in God's eyes. Even those who live with a moral compass, apart from Christ, are only producing self-righteousness.

Our feet can easily get dirty from walking in this world, which is why Jesus taught us to wash each other's feet (John 13:10). Our Lord Jesus is the One who cleanses our feet, but we must humble ourselves enough to let Him. It's not easy to show our dirty feet to Him, but we must overcome the shame and allow Him to wash us. Remember how Peter responded, *"Lord, not just my feet but my hands and my head as well"* (John 13:9 NIV)—this is how we must come to Jesus, willing to let Him cleanse all of us.

Confessing our sins and letting Jesus wash our feet is key to intimacy with Him. As 1 John 1:9 (NKJV) reminds us, *"If we confess our sins, He is faithful and just to forgive us our sins and to cleanse us from all unrighteousness."*

When the priest was commanded to sprinkle the blood on his right big toe, it was to make his feet holy. As priests of God, everything we do should be holy. To work in a holy way means recognizing that our strength comes from the blood of Jesus, not from ourselves.

Applying the blood to our feet means that everything we do must be covered by the blood. Our actions should always be under the blood; and after every deed, we must wash our feet again in His blood. Every step we take should be in the awareness of the blood that has been shed for us.

Laying hands on the animal's head was a symbolic transfer of sin onto the animal. The sacrificial laws were given by God Himself. Knowing the glory of the Cross but ignoring the blood is a shame to the Cross. Believers who are saved have already shed their own blood on the altar, whether visibly or invisibly.

> *But you are a chosen people, a royal priesthood, a holy nation, God's special possession, that you may declare the praises of him*

> *who called you out of darkness into his wonderful light* (1 Peter 2:9 NIV).

So we need to ask, is the blood sprinkled on my ears, on my hands, and on my feet? This is the life of a priest—a life covered in the blood of Jesus, set apart for His purposes. Only through the blood can we hear His Word, work for His glory, and walk in holiness.

# 10

# SAVED TO WORSHIP AND SAVE SOULS

What's next?

What do we do after we are saved? Who do we become after we surrender to Jesus? We become worshipers! You and I were originally created by God to worship Him! After meeting Jesus Christ, my heart was on fire and alive in and for Him. All the fear that I had as a Buddhist, or a non-Christian, was gone. It was replaced by supernatural boldness to speak to anyone, anywhere, anytime! I had dreams of seeing Jesus rapture me and demons leaving my life. Every day I became healthier and stronger by the grace of God, and I was ready to go back to normal life again, or so I thought.

You have probably heard the saying, "Do you want to know how to make God laugh? Tell Him your life plans." He already has the perfect, good, and acceptable plan for you if you only let Him move in your life (Romans 12:2-3). The key is surrender. When I was a new born-again Christian, I didn't know any of this yet. I wasn't a disciple at that time, but with my experience of seeing Heaven and hell during my near-death experience and in dreams, I was ready to tell everyone about Jesus and the Gospel! (See Romans 1:16.)

In the first few months of being saved, my insomnia, anxiety, and depression gradually disappeared, and I was deeply grateful for the believers from Grace Ministries International who visited me weekly. They always brought food and foundational Bible study materials. I began falling in love with God's Word and His Church, and it was during this time that my dream to become a pastor started to form.

Encouraged by church members and pastors from Grace Church, I went to a nearby prayer mountain in Corona, California, seeking to receive power from on high and draw closer to Jesus. Initially, I thought receiving Jesus was all there was to Christianity. But at the prayer mountain, where a Spirit-filled pastor named Pastor Oh led services three times a day, I learned there was more—I could also receive the baptism of the Holy Spirit.

In the morning and evening services, we always prayed after a time of praise and preaching. I would hear many older men and women praying in strange languages and sounds. It was in one of Pastor Oh's sermons that I first learned this was what Christians call "praying in tongues." I had been saved by the Gospel, by surrendering to Jesus, but I wasn't yet baptized in the Holy Spirit. I longed for the gift of tongues that first year after meeting Jesus in the fall of 1998.

"Father God, please let me speak in tongues! It sounds so heavenly, and I would love to pray to You in tongues like the apostle Paul did and as these Christians do today! Please don't pass me by!" And sure enough, on November 20, 1998, I was baptized in the Holy Spirit. I remember feeling heat and fire going through my body as Pastor Oh laid his hands on my head, just as he did for everyone who wanted prayer. But that night was different. I began speaking in tongues after rolling on the ground from the fire of the Holy Spirit. I didn't know such spiritual experiences were real, but later I discovered that many Spirit-filled Christians had similar experiences.

Acts 1:8 speaks of receiving power from on high to be His witnesses. Why do some Christians not witness or lack boldness in evangelism? I believe it's because they have not yet received the baptism of the Holy Spirit—the power from Heaven Jesus speaks of in Acts 1:8! You too can receive this bold power for Jesus, when you simply ask in Jesus' name to the Father!

## THE POWER FROM HEAVEN

I began speaking in tongues from that day on, and it was such a joy! At first, I had no idea what I was saying, so I would pray with my mind while speaking in tongues, asking God, "What am I saying, Lord?" The apostle Paul talks about asking God to interpret what we're praying in the Spirit, and I felt the Lord speak to my heart, saying, "You are praying, My son, let Your Kingdom come, and let Your will be done." Amen, Lord Jesus! That is the Lord's Prayer. I was so delighted and encouraged in my spirit to pray in the Spirit, and I began praying fervently every morning and night.

As I prayed daily at the prayer mountain during the fall and winter of 1998, a supernatural burden began to grow in me—a deep concern to see everyone around me repent and believe in Jesus. I felt stirred by God, and the passion to share what had happened to me with my friends, cousins, and even strangers was overwhelming. Back then, we still used cassette tapes, and CDs were just becoming popular, so I bought a tape recorder and started recording my testimony on cassette tapes. I would record a few tapes a day, and once I had a dozen or so, I started mailing them out and handing them to my friends, even to my ex-girlfriend.

They began calling me and asking, "Why did you change your religion, Steve?" "Jesus is real? How do you know?" These questions caught me off guard, and I didn't have the answers right away, but I knew one thing for sure—I believed my experience was real, and Jesus wanted them to know that He loves them and desires a relationship with them, too.

Though I didn't yet have answers to all their questions and wasn't trained in evangelism or apologetics, my heart burned with God's desire for sinners to come to Jesus through repentance and the power of the Gospel—the greatest news ever! It became clear that I needed to be trained to share more effectively. My boldness grew as I read the Bible more, and I became more confident in sharing with others.

I prayed, "Lord, save everyone on our campus! Only You can solve their problems and deliver them from spiritual blindness, emptiness, and judgment! Lord Jesus, have mercy." At the University of California, Irvine, many students were open to hearing the message. At times, the Holy Spirit would prompt me and some friends from our campus ministry to open-air preach in front of the lunch crowd or after classes, answering any questions they had.

To our surprise, many Christians came up to us afterward and shared that they felt encouraged and empowered to share the Gospel themselves. However, many rejected the Gospel as well. We simply kept sharing; it is not our job to judge nonbelievers or to determine the timing of someone's salvation. God can save anyone and He has the perfect timing!

As we saw people repenting and accepting Jesus, visiting our local churches, and attending our campus ministry worship nights, we became even more encouraged. We joined forces with other campus ministries—Asian American Christian Fellowship, Crossroads Campus Ministries, Campus Crusade for Christ (now called CRU), and more—and launched the "Reach Every Anteater" evangelism campaign, with the goal of reaching every student on campus for Jesus. It became the heartbeat of my time at UC Irvine. All the glory belongs to God for the salvation, healing, and miracles that took place there through us as we made ourselves available. The key wasn't ability; it was availability. As God says in His Word, *"Not by might nor by power, but by My Spirit!"* (Zechariah 4:6 NIV).

## IN "FIRST LOVE" WITH JESUS

> *Jesus replied: "'Love the Lord your God with all your heart and with all your soul and with all your mind.' This is the first and greatest commandment. And the second is like it: 'Love your neighbor as yourself'"* (Matthew 22:37-39 NIV).

Jesus places the greatest emphasis on the first commandment—the greatest commandment—and in the book of Revelation, He tells the church at Ephesus that they have left their first love and need to return to it:

> *Nevertheless I have this against you, that you have left your first love. Remember therefore from where you have fallen; repent and do the first works, or else I will come to you quickly and remove your lampstand from its place—unless you repent* (Revelation 2:4-5 NKJV).

The greatest commandment in the Bible is to love the Lord your God with all your heart, mind, soul, and strength (Matthew 22:37). But why is this so? It is because the Lord loves you with all His heart, mind, soul, and strength. He loves His creation, especially humankind, calling us sons, daughters, and even friends (John 15:14).

> *Greater love has no one than this, than to lay down one's life for his friends. You are My friends if you do whatever I command you. No longer do I call you servants, for a servant does not know what his master is doing; but I have called you friends, for all things that I heard from My Father I have made known to you* (John 15:13-15 NKJV).

Now, back to first love. I clearly remember when I first encountered Jesus Christ—my heart was warm, softened, my spirit awakened, my health restored, and joy filled my heart and mind in ways I had never known before. I was beyond grateful. He paid the price, and I was a new creation! Even the trees seemed to praise God, the birds, too, and every person I saw felt so precious, valuable, and lovable.

God allowed me to get a glimpse of His heart, and my heart began to align more and more with Jesus' heart by His grace. Psalm 73:25 (NKJV), *"Whom have I in heaven but You? And there is none upon the earth that I desire besides You,"* became my life verse, my favorite.

I longed and prayed for others to experience the same love from our Father in Christ Jesus through the Gospel.

Jesus was grieved that the Ephesian church had left their first love. Have you left your first love? Jesus' remedy for returning to that first love is clear: *"Remember therefore from where you have fallen; repent and do the first works, or else I will come to you quickly and remove your lampstand from its place—unless you repent."* I regularly repent of two things I've done—or more accurately, two things I've failed to do. The first is not loving God with all my heart, mind, soul, and strength. The second is not believing in the Word of God, the inerrant Word of God, with all my heart, 100 percent.

For the Church, for me, to return to our first love, we must repent of not loving God. Only then will Jesus fill us with His love again, or give us the capacity and grace to obey Him by His Word and Spirit. And when that happens, we can serve God again with a fresh sense of awe, wonder, and gratitude. Even as the wickedness around us increases in the last days, we can grow more and more in our ability to love.

Love is the purpose behind all of God's commandments. Keeping the first and second commandments—to love God and to love our neighbors as ourselves—fulfills all other commandments.

> *Love does no harm to a neighbor. Therefore love is the fulfillment of the law* (Romans 13:10 NIV).

Returning to our first love with Jesus, receiving the Kingdom of God with childlike faith, gives us the heart and ability to love our neighbors as ourselves. First love with Jesus is everything. We can always return to it by giving all of our hearts to Jesus again, saying no to the things of this world.

> *Do not love the world or anything in the world. If anyone loves the world, love for the Father is not in them. For everything in the world—the lust of the flesh, the lust of the eyes, and the pride*

*of life—comes not from the Father but from the world. The world and its desires pass away, but whoever does the will of God lives forever* (1 John 2:15-17 NIV).

First love with Jesus is the heartbeat of the Christian life, and keeping Jesus at the center of our hearts as Lord with passionate love is what it means to truly walk with Him. His love redeemed us and His love delivered us from judgment, eternal fire, and torment! I am so grateful sometimes just to be alive! My ambitions, goals, greed, even ministry goals do not matter in comparison to meditating on and thanking Jesus for His love! He deserves all our time, talents, treasure, past, present, and future now!

I attend and serve at Jesus Center (www.jesuscenter.com) where Pastor Daniel Park is the senior pastor. I am so grateful for this family, my church family, as many if not all of them are in love with Jesus. Ministry and service to community overflows from this love. This is a healthy church, warm, diligent, Spirit-filled, and always back in first love with Jesus.

First is ministry, from small to big, to small and pure, and now to the nations and end-time next generation! Everything is called to serve God. However, Pastor Jeff Jorg, the president of Gateway Seminary, in his book *Is God Calling Me?* distinguishes between three types of calling: 1) the universal call to Christian service for all believers; 2) a general call to ministry leadership; 3) and a specific call to a ministry assignment.

I was first called in 1998, the year I was saved, through the universal call, where I served in areas including welcoming and evangelism. As I grew in the Lord and in the Word of God, I received a general call to ministry leadership, which led me to serve on staff with campus ministries and a local church. After graduating from college, I enrolled at Talbot Seminary, as many do when they feel a specific call to ministry. Talbot is part of Biola University, founded by R.A. Torrey, a man well-respected for his knowledge of God and His Word.

I was excited to start seminary in 2004, imagining ministry to be filled with relaxing moments at the beach, sipping pineapple juice while reading the Bible and preparing sermons, with everyone shouting "Amen!" as they were set on fire for Jesus. But the reality was quite the opposite. For the first time in my life, I began to feel depression and fatigue again, like I had before I met Jesus. I left my home church, Grace Church, seeking a new assignment from God to grow and live by faith. I believe God, in His sovereignty, allowed this to happen, but it was a very difficult season in my life, a season when God began His training in me. Our Christian walk has seasons, and this was the beginning of learning how to die more to myself.

## A NEW SEASON

Seminary life was tough for me. The homework, especially the Greek and Hebrew assignments, were time-consuming, and with pastoring a small local church on top of it all, the toll was real. I began to see why some people refer to seminary as "cemetery." Even though I was preaching every Sunday for the Lord Jesus—what I believe is the highest calling in Christian service, besides intercession and evangelism—my heart felt empty and tired.

After a few years of spiritual dryness, I began to cry out to God in desperation: "God, I don't feel You anymore. Where are You? Are You not pleased with our service for You? Jesus, though I experienced Heaven and hell, my heart is dry. How is this possible?" Some church members were also critical of me. Some said I was too radical, others accused me of favoritism, and some just didn't care. People came and went, but I give glory to God that despite my shortcomings, He raised up leaders for the Gospel, some of whom even went on to seminary themselves.

During this season, I learned that *"Unless the Lord builds the house, they labor in vain who build it; unless the Lord guards the city, the watchman stays awake in vain"* (Psalm 127:1 NKJV). The works that God did lasted, and as our friends moved to other states for ministry and seminary, or to larger churches to serve, we had the joy of seeing their growth. I, too, was called to another church during this time. Our ministry in Koreatown, Los Angeles, was not easy, but there were young, fired-up believers there, and we were right in the middle of the city. Every Sunday, I had the privilege of meeting with 40 to 50 college students and young adults, and my friend, Simon from Talbot, served as the youth pastor with me. Though I was still tired and dealing with insomnia as a seminary student, I experienced more joy than before as we labored together for a few years.

Another church in Irvine, California, asked me to pastor there, and we became partner churches, laboring together for the next generation. We even adopted a building in a project housing zone nearby and saw homeless people, prostitutes, and others oppressed by society set free and born again in Christ. We went on mission trips to China, Thailand, and even Hawaii, preaching the Gospel with local partner churches. My first love and joy in Jesus began to emerge again as I saw the Lord moving.

I wasn't physically fully recovered from the accident in 1998, nor was I taking care of my health very well as a young, single pastor-in-training, but I loved being with the next generation and my friends in Jesus. Life wasn't as lonely, but my lack of mentoring and maturity in Christ led me to experience spiritual highs and lows during this season. Unlike my peers at seminary, many of whom grew up in church or in Christian households, I grew up in a Buddhist home, filled with various worldly experiences. But through every temptation and battle, I can honestly say that Jesus helped and delivered me.

I learned that being tempted is one thing, but submitting to and committing sin is another. God does not tempt anyone; rather, we are tempted by our own evil desires (James 1:13-14). Even though we're saved, I realized that the old nature is still lurking, just as Paul describes in Romans 7 and 8. He says in 1 Corinthians 15:31 (NKJV), *"I affirm, by the boasting in you which I have in Christ Jesus our Lord, I die daily."*

I believe the apostle Paul was referring to dying to his old nature, his selfish nature, and his self-made agenda as Jesus became Lord over him each day. He didn't say he died weekly or monthly, but daily. Jesus Himself too made this clear in the Gospels:

> *Then He said to them all, "If anyone desires to come after Me, let him deny himself, and take up his cross daily, and follow Me. For whoever desires to save his life will lose it, but whoever loses his life for My sake will save it. For what profit is it to a man if he gains the whole world, and is himself destroyed or lost?"* (Luke 9:23-25 NKJV)

Why do we need to die daily and deny ourselves to follow Jesus if our old nature is already gone? So we gain our souls and say no to the world's false promises of glitter and temporary glory. Our old sinful nature still has the potential to rise again. Christianity, the cross, is about experiencing God's love and grace, yes, but it is also about training ourselves. It is about experiencing Heaven, but also denying ourselves and losing our life for Jesus and the Gospel's sake. This is the call to discipleship.

After we are saved, we must be discipled, plug into the local church family, and serve. Having a heart of honor greatly helps in this. We also launched a School of Ministers[4] and the first topic we cover is honor. John Bevere's book, *Honor's Reward,* is highly recommended if we are to receive God's full reward and plans for our lives. No matter how imperfect a church or a company we work for is, we are called to

---

4 For more information, visit www.schoolofministers.com.

honor, unless of course, the church is teaching heretical doctrine and the leaders not living as godly examples.

Does your church preach this on a regular basis? Or is it another feel-good service that focuses on prosperity and having Heaven on earth? These blessings come as a result of denying ourselves by His grace. Grace means Jesus empowers us to obey and live holy lives—not just to have "life insurance" through the Gospel. Paul himself writes in 1 Corinthians 9:27 (NKJV), *"But I discipline my body and bring it into subjection, lest, when I have preached to others, I myself should become disqualified."*

Fasting, morning prayer, quiet times, reading, evangelism, missions, and even learning to rest became essential parts of my Christian walk. While others preached that we are saved and free, I wanted to understand what that truly meant according to the boundaries set by the Word of God.

I came across a book titled *The True Bounds of Christian Freedom* by Pastor Samuel Bolton, written in the early 17th century, which deeply impacted my understanding. In short, I learned that biblical grace makes Jesus Lord, and holiness is not an option. Grace empowers us to obey, and many can claim to love Jesus, but true fruit is seen in doing the will of the Father. Holiness is a real characteristic of being a follower of Christ. We can make mistakes, but we must repent immediately and surrender. It might be hard to surrender, but it's even harder not to!

Paul warns us in 1 Corinthians 6:9-11:

> *Do you not know that the unrighteous will not inherit the kingdom of God? Do not be deceived. Neither fornicators, nor idolaters, nor adulterers, nor homosexuals, nor sodomites, nor thieves, nor covetous, nor drunkards, nor revilers, nor extortioners will inherit the kingdom of God. And such were some of you. But you were washed, but you were sanctified, but you were justified in the name of the Lord Jesus and by the Spirit of our God.*

After about four years of ministry and seminary, just as I was about to graduate, the senior pastor at Grace Church called me back to serve the next generation. I gladly said yes, and in 2008, I returned to my home church—the place where I was saved, baptized in water and the Spirit—and began serving alongside another pastor with about 300 youth students. I felt a sense of rest and satisfaction again, but it was short-lived as the demands and expectations of the ministry doubled. Despite the challenges, I was deeply grateful to be there, and our focus on missions, evangelism, and prayer was worth it all.

The motto you'll find if you walk into the church is: *1. Missions is warfare 2. Missions is prayer 3. Missions is martyrdom.* Hallelujah! This is not the popular prosperity Gospel message—it is the reality, how the world really works. Through this one local church, Jesus planted 10,000 churches, baptized 1 million souls, all documented, and I was honored to be part of that. I was also ordained as a pastor after completing 21 days of liquid fasting and graduating from Talbot Seminary. I thought my training was over, but God had another season of training in store, teaching me that life is not about me—it is all about Jesus, others second, and me last.

## TRUE REPENTANCE—A DAILY BATTLE FOR THE CROSS

The daily Christian life is what gives a repented sinner, turned saint, the assurance of salvation. Having the assurance of salvation, in turn, gives us amazing inner peace, peace with God, peace with others, boldness, assurance in prayer, and also a greater sense of purpose. The number-one goal in Christianity is to go to Heaven, and for pastors to bring their pasture to Heaven. Nothing else matters in this life, and of course, in all of eternity.

I start my day with prayer, thanksgiving, and praise. Quiet time also helps me remember verses and think about God throughout the day. When we do this, our priorities shift toward God and His Kingdom, turning the day into joy. According to God's presence and the Word, we can be filled with joy. To get rid of depression or distractions, we don't simply turn away from them or focus on avoiding them. We need to enter into the Lord's presence. There, He heals us, takes away our trials, and lifts the weight of depression and useless distractions.

I have a gratitude journal for this purpose. When I am feeling down or discouraged, I open it and start writing down everything I'm thankful for. I re-read past entries, and before long, I forget why I was feeling down. Gratitude is a powerful weapon. It shifts our focus and changes our mindset, enabling us to focus on what we can do, rather than what we can't.

When it feels like no one is on your side, when everything seems hopeless or when you're struggling with suicidal thoughts, I want to remind you of this: The Lord has a plan for you. Even your pain is part of His plan and His will to use you. Part of that plan is learning obedience. Hebrews 5:8 says that even Jesus Himself learned obedience through suffering. Not all suffering is God-ordained, but through all suffering, we can learn obedience and gratitude. And it will not last forever. It is going to be okay.

I can say this with confidence because I have experienced great suffering myself. Yet, I know that the greatest sufferings are the greatest blessings in disguise, and they are all part of the Lord's plans for me, and for you. The Lord allowed me to see hell and showed me Heaven in His mercy and love. This is why I have such a passion for those who suffer from depression and suicidal thoughts. I want to tell you this: The reason Jesus allowed suffering is twofold. First, to save us. Second, to use our story to save others who are suffering in the same way. He wants to use your story to show others how He has saved you through your suffering. Trust in His Word completely. Let go and stop worrying.

After the Covid quarantine began, the Lord reignited my faith and passion. We began praying every morning, and as of today, we've completed 1521 consecutive prayers (not counting Sundays). The word the Lord gave us during this time was twofold: *First, wake up My Church. Second, fill My Church with holiness until I return.*

My heart for the Church began to burn with passion. Whenever I meet believers, I first think about how to kindle the fire in their hearts, and how to be kindled by them as well. Everyone has a passion for something. If that passion isn't directed toward the Lord, it will surely go elsewhere—whether it be sports, the pleasures of this world, or even laziness.

Through more prayer, the Lord's word became even stronger: Let yourself go for Jesus. Let your passion burn for Jesus. Let no sigh come from your mouth, but be like the five wise virgins waiting for the Lord's return. If we do not, we will miss our one chance, and only regret will remain. Ignite your passion for Jesus now, today. Do not just be hot on the outside. My prayer for all of us is that by allowing Jesus to take over every part of us, we will burn inside and overflow with His love and power everywhere we go, to give Jesus' life to everyone.

For those who are not yet saved, the Lord says, *"Come to Me, all you who are weary and burdened, and I will give you rest. Take My yoke upon you and learn from Me, for I am gentle and humble in heart, and you will find rest for your souls. For My yoke is easy, and My burden is light"* (Matthew 11:28-30 NKJV).

My heart beats for the Church and for lost souls, evangelism. We are given a once-in-a-lifetime opportunity, every single day. Our lives will pass, but the life of Christ is eternal. Eternal life is knowing Jesus and the Father personally (John 17:3). Do you know God personally, or just from afar religiously? We are privileged to witness the Lord's work in us and through us.

I hope the Church no longer remains silent on matters of right and wrong from God's perspective. Silent churches must wake up and join the work of the harvest. *"The harvest is plentiful, but the workers are few. Therefore ask the Lord of the harvest to send out workers into His harvest field"* (Luke 10:2 NIV). He will do it when we pray with childlike faith. It is time to bring the Church outside the four walls. So we go to mosques, Walmarts, malls, open-air preach at restaurants, in the streets, carry gospel tracts, pray for people, pray for deliverance, healing, and invite people to church, follow up, and equip other churches. That is why Revive The Nations ministry was created as well, to equip local churches to evangelize daily, not just once a year during annual missions trips. Our neighborhoods, where we live daily, is the mission field.

However, there was a time when I too felt lonely, confused, weak, and doubted the need for surrendering my all to Jesus. However, through prayers and personal encounters with Him, the love of healthy churches, and fatherly and motherly mentors, I completely regained my fervent faith. I now understand deeply that I am a child of the Lord God, that He will never leave me nor forsake me, and that I have eternal life. I am precious in His sight, and I am living the life I am most grateful for. It is the life Jesus promised, life to the fullest (John 10:10). I am thankful to God for simply being able to breathe! My conscience is clear, and I am bold to pray before God and speak to anyone in wisdom for Jesus. I pray you too can have a pure conscience, peaceful heart, diligent spiritual life, and bold faith, knowing you will not go to hell—you will go to Heaven when you die.

There is no need any more for selfish or worldly goals or ambitions. I no longer desire anything but a life of walking with Jesus. No matter how many people I care about and come to know, our Lord Jesus always come first. And this should be true for you as well. He should be our highest priority—what pleases Him is what matters most in our daily lives. Life is all about Jesus and what He desires and is pleased with.

We worship the living God now—the only One who is eternal and immortal, the One who alone deserves all glory, praise, and worship. Never forget: The Lord who created the people you love, always comes first, before anyone or anything else. We love our families, neighbors, and even our enemies now, but Jesus is first place in everything. I pray you stop fearing about going to hell and rather have a warm welcome to Heaven as a result of your living the life of the Cross, surrendered to Jesus, and walking on the narrow path every day of your life, not just on Sundays.

# 11

# WALKING THROUGH THE NARROW DOOR TO HEAVEN

I did not share much about the details of my ministry during and after seminary, in both small and large churches, on the streets, or during open-air preaching. Nevertheless, from the beginning of my walk with Christ, I was baptized in the Holy Spirit, had visions of Heaven and hell by God's grace, and encountered Jesus in a very radical way. I did not choose the type of Christianity I was introduced to, I simply heard and saw how good God is, and I knew I could not shrink back from the call because of the fear of unbelievers, criticism from others, or opposition from legalistic Christians. When we surrender to God above people and desire to please Him, God looks down from Heaven to see whether or not He can use us. The narrow road of life involves being available to serve God anytime, anywhere, and in any way to anyone.

My testimony became known to my friends in seminary, and they, along with their friends in local churches, began to invite me to share my story of seeing hell. Initially, I did not go into detail about my suicide attempt, as I still felt a bit of shame about my past story. However, after the Covid outbreak, I felt the grace and call of God to share more openly, and in greater detail, the journey He has taken me on.

From 2004 to 2012, God used me in revival ministry, and I was both grateful and excited for every opportunity, despite still struggling with health issues and insomnia. I knew the power of prayer, but God waited until after I was married to fully heal me—ridding me of insomnia and restoring my health. When I met my wife, Goeun Kim, during Thanksgiving weekend in 2016, I knew she was the one God sent for me. Through thick and thin, she stuck by me, as we have been married for eight years now. As pastor Tim Keller says in his marriage book, marriage sanctified and humbled me. I wish I had been married sooner, and pray that all young men and women seeking to serve God get married early and not wait too long, for two is better than one, and through marriage we learn that life is not about "me." It is both boring and barren to live for oneself.

## REVIVALS—THEN AND NOW

Every revival I was called to involved summer or winter youth retreats, evangelism rallies, or all-church events aimed at calling people back to God. I read about the power of intercession through the autobiographies and biographies of giants like Charles Finney, John Hyde, John Wesley, George Whitefield, D.L. Moody, George Muller, Reinhard Bonnke, and Wesley Duewel. Through these accounts, I began to see how God used His people to awaken the Church, His people. It became clear to me that God does not just work through angels in the Bible, but mostly through people—His people.

What an honor to be used by Him. In 2024 alone, I preached and shared at 95 churches and ministry interviews, some almost a week long, others a few hours. He stirs us up to do His will, and He even uses nonbelievers to guide and bless His people at times. God desires all people to have faith that moves mountains, and pure love that never gives up on people. We are Spirit-possessed, not just Spirit-led.

As 1 Peter 2:9-10 (NKJV) says:

> *But you are a chosen generation, a royal priesthood, a holy nation, His own special people, that you may proclaim the praises of Him*

> *who called you out of darkness into His marvelous light; who once were not a people but are now the people of God, who had not obtained mercy but now have obtained mercy.*

We are the recipients of God's mercy, and as we love and give to others, we become His hands and feet, bringing glory to the Father.

Matthew 5:14-16 (NKJV) reminds us:

> *You are the light of the world. A city that is set on a hill cannot be hidden. Nor do they light a lamp and put it under a basket, but on a lampstand, and it gives light to all who are in the house. Let your light so shine before men, that they may see your good works and glorify your Father in heaven.*

Though I was not a big "general" like those described in Roberts Liardon's book *God's Generals,* every time I went to preach at revival and evangelism events, I always took intercessors with me. If they were not available, I would text my pastors, friends, and my mother, asking them to pray for me, and the church where I was visiting to minister. God does not want our testimonies or the Gospel hidden. Our job is to show up and share the Word of God, prayed up, and He will do the rest.

Every event filled with prayer and fasting resulted in students and adults repenting in tears, receiving Jesus Christ, receiving the baptism of the Holy Spirit and tongues, and being healed and delivered. It took a toll on my body, but as a saved man who should be in hell, I did not care. I was fully available.

By God's grace and guidance, more doors opened for me, and I traveled to places including Korea, San Francisco, New York, Ohio, Oklahoma, Virginia, Toronto, Canada, London, San Diego, Cambodia, Indonesia, Thailand, China, Myanmar, and Seoul. God sent me throughout parts of the United States and world to share the Gospel, to testify about His grace that leads people from hell to Heaven. I made myself available to anyone who wanted the truth. Worship is not about people, nor is revival the result of people's efforts. As Leonard Ravenhill said, "Revival is when God gets so sick and tired of being misrepresented that He shows Himself." He also said, "The only reason we don't have revival is because we are willing to live without it." We must pray for revival; but ultimately, it is up to God to send it. Let us be sent, and not be ones who went.

R.A. Torrey perfectly sums it up: "Every true revival...has had its earthly origin in prayer." Whether we are talking about the early Church, the Reformation, or the Great Awakenings in America and other nations, united prayer was the catalyst for revival.

For a few years, I became fascinated with the topic of revival, and by God's grace, I met Pastor Elijah Kim, a revivalist and scholar who came to America from the Philippines. He introduced me to revival expert scholars such as William McLoughlin, Harvey Cox, Allan Anderson, Vishal Mangalwadi, and Robert Oh. He even asked me to translate his own scholarly work, *The Rise of the Global South,* which took more than a year to finish. During those years of interacting with him, I learned so much about the history of revival in the Church and throughout the world. His works on intercession, revival, and awakenings deeply impacted me and opened my eyes to the reality of the need for prayer, the willingness to lay down one's life, and the spiritual diligence required to do the Lord's work.

I began to understand that God is always ready to move and visit His people, but the question is—do we, as the Church, truly desire it? Will we be grateful, or will we become burdened, cold, or burned out? Lasting revival only happens when we do our part—just like in any meaningful relationship that bears good fruit, such as a marriage. I saw how other church leaders in both conservative and charismatic circles sought and experienced revival, transforming entire congregations and cities, as documented in George Otis Jr.'s *Transformations* series. I lived with this hunger for revival, even having some awkward conversations with fellow believers who weren't interested.

Seeing revival unfold, watching churches pray and evangelize again, brought me so much joy. Despite being physically weak during those years, I experienced the joy of first love being restored as I saw young people come to Jesus. At that time, nothing mattered more than doing God's will on earth.

I didn't expect to live a normal or comfortable life until I was married. And everything changed when I met my wife, Goeun Kim, during Thanksgiving weekend in 2016. My over-spiritual zeal and my tendency to spiritualize all aspects of life had to shift. I became a bi-vocational pastor, as my mentors advised me to get a job to provide for my wife. First Timothy 5:8 (NIV) says, *"Anyone who does not provide for their relatives, and especially for their own household, has denied the faith and is worse than an unbeliever."*

I had to humble myself, stepping down from the "ivory tower" of full-time ministry, and learn to live a normal, married life. However, the joy of marriage far outweighed the cost. I wish someone had told me to get married earlier! My wife came from a godly, well-educated family, and I am constantly grateful that she chose to marry a ministry-focused pastor like me. She truly became the greatest gift from God—aside from my salvation in Christ—and her presence also helped restore my health. My insomnia was healed, and I learned to enjoy working in the corporate world. My mentor, Timothy Oh of Kingdom Business Redeemers, taught me that, "My work is His message." To my surprise, ministry also became more joyful, and I began to see lasting fruit. Being able to provide for my wife became a calling, and I found great joy in it as well.

C.T. Studd's words ring true: "Only one life, it will soon be past, only what's done for Christ will last."

On the topic of mentors and revival, I believe we need to learn to honor spiritual leaders and the history of the Christian Church. We are not starting something brand-new—nothing is truly new under the sun. For 2,000 years, countless godly men and women have walked with Jesus and shown us how to live godly lives. Having personal spiritual mentors is invaluable, though it may not always be possible in every season of life. Sometimes, the answer to our prayers and breakthroughs is not far away in the future, but right in front of us, in the Kingdom of God that is near. Honoring the people in our lives is the answer to many of life's challenges. When we see Christ in one another, it brings immense joy and peace.

As 2 Corinthians 5:16-17 (NKJV) says: *"Therefore, from now on, we regard no one according to the flesh. Even though we have known Christ according to the flesh, yet now we know Him thus no longer. Therefore, if anyone is in Christ, he is a new creation; old things have passed away; behold, all things have become new."*

God is near, not far away. Jeremiah 23:23-24 (NKJV) declares: "'Am I a God near at hand,' says the Lord, 'And not a God afar off? Can anyone hide himself in secret places, So I shall not see him?' says the Lord; 'Do I not fill heaven and earth?' says the Lord."

God works through people, and He often works through your godly family, local church community, and friends in Christ. Mentors, spiritual books, and Christian leaders are essential for those called to serve the Church, and we are grateful for every friend and partner who helps advance the Kingdom of God during our time here on earth.

For revival to happen, the Church must fast and pray. We must obey God, say no to the flesh, and turn away from the world so that the love of the Father can dwell in our hearts. If we lay everything down at Jesus' feet and focus on His business, He will take care of ours (Matthew 6:33). We do not and will not preach the prosperity Gospel, but we preach Jesus Christ as not just Savior but as Lord.

United prayer in the Church, and between churches will bring revival. A lasting revival, with fruit that endures, will come as we continue to choose Jesus and life. For us, Jesus is more than enough. God can touch a button in our brain to release endorphins stronger than any chemical that scientists have created, and the joy of salvation can be restored, and remain with us always.

We can choose to soften our hearts, love the unlovable, forgive the unforgivable, and bless the unblessable. We can hang out with the lowly because we too are nothing without Jesus. We serve those who can never repay us in this life, for Jesus will reward us for life eternal! Then, when is the right time for revival in your life, your church, and your city? It is now. It is today!

Second Corinthians 6:2 (NKJV) reminds us: *"For He says: 'In an acceptable time I have heard you, and in the day of salvation I have helped you.' Behold, now is the accepted time; behold, now is the day of salvation."*

In Isaiah 11, God reveals the third person of the Trinity, the Holy Spirit, and highlights His sevenfold nature, showing us His traits and personalities. What exactly is the Trinity? The Trinity is described clearly in 1 John 5:7 (NKJV): *"For there are three that bear witness in heaven: the Father, the Word, and the Holy Spirit; and these three are one."* Jesus, as the Word (John 1), is one with the Father and the Holy Spirit, together making up the three Persons of the Triune God.

Isaiah 11:1-2 (NKJV) provides further insight into the Holy Spirit:

> *There shall come forth a Rod from the stem of Jesse, and a Branch shall grow out of his roots. The Spirit of the Lord shall rest upon Him, the Spirit of wisdom and understanding, the Spirit of counsel and might, the Spirit of knowledge and of the fear of the Lord.*

In many developed nations, churches may focus on teaching about the Father and the Son but can sometimes overlook the Holy Spirit. On the mission field or in churches where there is more vibrancy and freedom in the Spirit, the conversation about the Holy Spirit flourishes. The truth is, no Christian can live a joy-filled, victorious life without being filled with the Holy Spirit. To be full of the Spirit is to be full of faith, and to be full of faith, we need to be filled with the Holy Spirit. How do we become full of the Holy Spirit? It's simple yet profound—by asking God the Father.

> *If you then, being evil, know how to give good gifts to your children, how much more will your heavenly Father give the Holy Spirit to those who ask Him!* (Luke 11:13 NKJV)

The fullness of the Holy Spirit is given to those who ask and pray, not automatically to everyone who is saved. Salvation is a one-time decision, but being filled with the Holy Spirit is a daily choice. This is why godly discipline is so important in the Christian walk. Throughout Scripture, those whom God used powerfully were people of prayer. The apostles had dedicated times of prayer, and even Jesus would often withdraw to quiet places, both at the start and end of His day, to pray and spend time with the Father.

There are testimonies from ex-satanists, such as John Ramirez, who share how they were able to attack and defeat Christians who didn't pray enough. Through prayer and spending time with the Holy Spirit, both individually and in community, we get to know the sevenfold Spirit of God. There's no greater privilege than walking with the Holy Spirit, than walking with God Himself.

Now, let's take a deeper look at Isaiah 11:1-2:

> *There shall come forth a Rod from the stem of Jesse, and a Branch shall grow out of his roots. The Spirit of the Lord shall rest upon Him, the Spirit of wisdom and understanding, the Spirit of counsel and might, the Spirit of knowledge and of the fear of the Lord.*

The *"Rod from the stem of Jesse"* and the *"Branch"* refer to Jesus Christ. Isaiah, in the spirit, prophesied that Jesus would arise from Israel and be filled with the Holy Spirit. The *"Spirit of the Lord"* in this passage refers to the Holy Spirit.

## WISDOM AND FEAR OF THE LORD

The Holy Spirit is filled with wisdom and understanding. But what is wisdom? We often think of wisdom as being efficient or morally sound, but God defines wisdom differently. Job 28:28 (NKJV) says, *"And to man He said, 'Behold, the **fear** of the Lord, that is wisdom, and to depart from evil is understanding.'"*

This "fear" is not about being afraid but about having a deep reverence and respect for God. It's a love-driven respect where we avoid sin—not just out of duty, but because we don't want to offend the One we love. While His perfect love casts out fear, the kind of fear we're talking about here is a holy awe that keeps us aligned with God's will and helps us to stay away from sin. It's this fear of the Lord that leads us to wisdom and understanding.

> *The fear of the Lord is the beginning of wisdom, and the knowledge of the Holy One is understanding* (Proverbs 9:10).

When we ask daily to be filled with the Holy Spirit, we become more intimate with the Holy One, gaining a deeper understanding of His heart and ways. Living a God-centered life, where Jesus is exalted in our worship and ministry, leads to wisdom and knowledge that truly last. What a privilege it is to fear God and have intimate knowledge of Him!

> *Wisdom and knowledge will be the stability of your times, and the strength of salvation; the fear of the Lord is His treasure* (Isaiah 33:6 NKJV).

In these uncertain times, do you long for stability? There's only one way to find it: *fear God and keep His commandments.* This is the essence of the Gospel—grace and truth. Jesus came to reveal the Father to us, and whoever has seen the Son has seen the Father. Stability is found when we align our hearts with the Lord's will and trust in His ways.

The Holy Spirit is also filled with counsel and might. God gives us godly counsel, and no counsel can prevail against His. He works in ways we can't fully understand, and He works all things for the good of those who love Him.

> *Now He who searches the hearts knows what the mind of the Spirit is, because He makes intercession for the saints according to the will of God. And we know that all things work together for good to those who love God, to those who are the called according to His purpose* (Romans 8:27-28 NKJV).

Do you need counsel for your life or a situation you're facing? Ask the Holy Spirit! Whether in politics, business, or church growth, He is willing and able to help—just ask and you will receive!

The Holy Spirit is also the Spirit of might. Sometimes, we plan, dream, and envision, but our flesh is weak. We grow weary with the demands of life—work, family, and everything in between. We try to execute, but fall short. That's when we need the Spirit of might. The Holy Spirit gives us supernatural strength to carry out God's will, no matter how challenging it might seem.

We live by faith, not by sight, trusting in the One for whom nothing is impossible. How can we tap into the Spirit of might when we feel weak or lacking?

> *For we do not have a High Priest who cannot sympathize with our weaknesses, but was in all points tempted as we are, yet without sin. Let us therefore come boldly to the throne of grace, that we may obtain mercy and find grace to help in time of need* (Hebrews 4:15-16 NKJV).

Jesus invites us to come boldly to the throne of grace—not timidly but confidently—knowing that we will receive mercy and grace in our time of need. The Spirit of might is given to those who pray boldly, with confidence. How do we know our prayers are answered? Simple—

> *For if our heart condemns us, God is greater than our heart, and knows all things. Beloved, if our heart does not condemn us, we have confidence toward God. And whatever we ask we receive from Him, because we keep His commandments and do those things that are pleasing in His sight* (1 John 3:20-22 NKJV).

Is there anything in your life that condemns you? Our conscience is our shield of faith, and if our hearts don't condemn us, we can have confidence toward God that He will answer our prayers. This confidence comes from obedience, for *obedience is the currency of Heaven*—Heaven operates on faith! You can't obey someone you don't trust, respect, or worship, so by keeping His commandments, we can have great confidence in prayer.

Our desire is to please Him, and when we abide in His love and keep His Word in us, we can approach Him with confidence, knowing that He delights in answering our prayers. His commandments aren't burdensome—they simply boil down to loving God and loving others. That's the heart of the law and the prophets, and it's how we walk in the Spirit of might.

## KNOWLEDGE AND UNDERSTANDING

The Holy Spirit is also the Spirit of knowledge and the fear of the Lord. We've already touched on the fear of the Lord and its importance in all aspects of life.

Then what is the difference between knowledge and understanding? Knowledge is knowing facts or truths—understanding goes deeper, seeking to understand why or how things were created. Knowledge is knowing who God is and how He created the heavens and the earth, while understanding is delving into how He made it all work together.

The greatest scientists, engineers, and inventors understood the mind of God and His creation. They didn't create their own world—they discovered how God's world works.

A.W. Tozer, a spiritual giant, only attended school up to the 5th grade. Yet his books, such as *The Pursuit of God*, are filled with profound insights that can change your life. Tozer was filled with the Holy Spirit, and as he studied literature, he became a better writer than many with advanced degrees. This is the power of the Holy Spirit!

When we allow ourselves to be filled with the sevenfold Spirit of God (see Isaiah 11:2), we grow in our understanding of Him and His creation. The more we seek Him, the more He takes us from glory to glory. Jesus desires to lead us deeper into the knowledge of God, and when we walk in the fullness of the Holy Spirit, we'll know Him like never before.

It is a journey of faith, obedience, and love—a journey that opens our hearts to the wisdom and might of the Holy Spirit. May we walk in that fullness, trusting in God to lead us through every season of life.

## TO REACH ONE MORE

Let's love and trust in Jesus alone! The purpose behind writing this book on hell didn't become clear to me until God touched my heart, just as He has touched millions of others—to reach one more for Jesus. King Solomon, the wisest man, warns us in Ecclesiastes 12:12 (NKJV), *"And further, my son, be admonished by these. Of making many books there is no end, and much study is wearisome to the flesh."*

The only time study and reading are truly worthwhile is when they draw us closer to Jesus and help us trust Him more. We can't live off of past testimonies, revelations, or knowledge alone. We need fresh, daily manna as spiritual beings—mind, heart, and body.

Every morning, God asks us the same question: *Do you trust Me?* And through trials and tests, as we grow into His image, our response should be, *"Yes, Lord Jesus! I completely trust in You!"* God is speaking to us today, right now.

> *Now the just* [righteous] *shall live by faith; but if anyone draws back, My soul has no pleasure in him* (Hebrews 10:38 NKJV).

*Drawing back* means not trusting God, or doubting Him. God deserves our trust. He is faithful, His mercies endure forever, and He is always trustworthy. We all face moments of unbelief or weakness, but that should not be the norm in our Christian walk. God refines our faith and takes us deeper, but faith is meant to grow in seasons.

God delights in our faith—He loves being trusted by His creation. His Kingdom, power, and glory belong to Him alone! The more I get to know God, the more I love Him. Life with God may not always be easy, but I love Him more this year than last, and the journey is amazing. As the beloved hymn states, "Amazing grace, how sweet the sound, that saved a wretch like me!"

There are events, diseases, and wars that forever change the world, and the book of Revelation makes it clear that difficult times are ahead for those living on earth. Jesus Himself called these times *"great tribulation, such as has not been since the beginning of the world until this time, no, nor ever shall be"* (Matthew 24:21 NKJV).

Nonetheless, we are not afraid. At Jesus Center, and Revive The Nations,[5] we talk often about the end times and why we must save one more soul for Jesus. Even though Covid shut down many churches in

5 For more information, visit www.allnationsjc.org.

2020, we planted small groups and churches during that time. God awakened us, revived our hearts, and we repented of living for ourselves. Together we declared, "Jesus, we want to love and trust You more! You are all we want, help us know You are near!" All day, every day, we want to be with Jesus.

The apostle Paul expressed this desire in Philippians 1:22-23 (NKJV): *"But if I live on in the flesh, this will mean fruit from my labor; yet what I shall choose I cannot tell. For I am hard-pressed between the two, having a desire to depart and be with Christ, which is far better."*

As a church, we love this verse. We are grateful for life on earth to bear fruit for Jesus, but we look forward to the day we'll see Him face to face—it will be far better. For unbelievers, death is a sad day, but for those of us who believe in Jesus, it's the better day.

With the "Great Reset" being planned by global leaders, the world is growing darker and more confusing. However, we know that the people of God will shine brighter than ever! We believe that God uses all things for the good of those who love Him. Covid awakened us spiritually and reignited our passion for the harvest. The field is level now—church size, pastor fame, and resources don't matter. We can all reach our neighbors, whether online, offline, or by planting small groups and churches everywhere we go.

## UNITED FOR THE KINGDOM

Churches across the world are uniting for Kingdom purposes like never before. Pastors and leaders are coming together to grow spiritually and to preach the Gospel, as we did at INLA4LA with Pastor Erwin and 120 other pastors in January 2025. Fulfilling the Great Commission as we walk in the Great Commandment has never been more urgent. Grace is available for us to obey. Jesus, we love You, worship You, and trust You completely! We live with the assurance of salvation and the faith that our prayers will be answered.

I pray you will make it a habit to read Matthew chapters 5–7, John chapters 14–17, and 1 John on a weekly basis, and of course, read the entire Bible regularly. These chapters show you how people who go to Heaven, and avoid hell, actually live daily. I pray you can read these chapters weekly and truly have Jesus and His Word abundantly dwell in your heart.

Do not let condemnation, fear, or worry take hold of you, nor anyone's opinion. As we grow closer to Jesus, His Word and His opinion will matter more than anything else. Of course, we must live in community, family, and accountability, but Jesus wants to be the center of every area of our lives—every moment, every day.

Are you ready to live the Spirit-filled, narrow road faith life and avoid the wide road of hell and destruction? God is calling each of us to do so today, because He loves us always and forever. Jesus is Lord!

Pastor Vlad Savchuk is a friend of mine whom I deeply respect for living the revival life, walking on the narrow road of life every day. He shares on his website prayers how to overcome fear.[6] The following is the first 10 of 30. Declare them out loud, not just think them. They are powerful, and they work because we are praying them in Jesus' name, and they all come from His Word the Bible!

Declare these ten declarations to overcome fear:

1. In the name of Jesus, I refuse to fear, for God has given me a spirit not of fear but of power, love, and a sound mind (2 Timothy 1:7).
2. I bind the spirit of fear in my life, in Jesus' name.
3. I break every evil covenant causing fear in my life, in Jesus' name.
4. I command every terror of the night inciting fear, to stop and leave my environment, in Jesus' name (Psalm 91:5).

6 www.pastorvlad.org.

5. You, spirit of fear, lose your hold upon my life and family, in Jesus' name.
6. I command all human agents using spirits of fear to terrify me to stumble and fall, in Jesus' name (Psalm 27:2).
7. The fear and terror of the unbelievers shall not be my lot, in Jesus' name (Isaiah 54:14).
8. My tomorrow is blessed by God; therefore, all spirits responsible for the fear of tomorrow, I bind you, in Jesus' name (Jeremiah 29:11).
9. My destiny is attached to God; I declare I will not fail, in Jesus' name (Jeremiah 29:11).
10. Every bondage that I am subjecting myself to by the spirit of fear, I break in Jesus' name.

## HOW TO KNOW JESUS MORE

Christians are saved by grace through faith (Ephesians 2:8-9), and we walk in faith (2 Corinthians 5:7). Only by faith in Christ are we made righteous (Romans 5:19). Paul further speaks regarding spiritual truth in Galatians 2:16 (ESV), *"We know that a person is not justified by works of the law but through faith in Jesus Christ, so we also have believed in Christ Jesus, in order to be justified by faith in Christ and not by works of the law, because by works of the law no one will be justified."* It is Christ's righteousness that saves us, and the only way to receive that gift is to trust in Him. *"Whoever believes in the Son has eternal life"* (John 3:36 ESV).

We can know Jesus more by putting God first. As my good friend Ben always says, "G1! JOY comes from putting Jesus first, others second, yourself last." I love that! Freedom comes when we let go and surrender to His will; and as we obey God, He reveals Himself to us more and more, and takes us indeed from glory to glory!

You can say the sinner's prayer and invite Jesus into your life. What is more important is afterward to forgive everyone who has ever wronged you, as the Lord has forgiven you, and get plugged in and serve in the local church. Though imperfect, do not be offended at other Christians or leaders, but rather discover what your calling is where God called you to be.

Be humble and disciple others. Do not say, "Just me and Jesus for the rest of my life." I have never seen people grow who live alone. Growth happens in community, imperfect relationships, and as we receive the love of Jesus from the church and other believers, and even nonbelievers.

Lord Jesus, I surrender all!

Lord Jesus, take over!

Lord Jesus, have Your way!

Lord Jesus, be my First Love!

Lord Jesus, have mercy on me!

Lord Jesus, help me!

Pray this prayer regularly and commit all of your life to Him! Read the Word every day, journal, and commit to a worship and church-centered life, as you evangelize passionately and regularly!

## VICTORY PRAYERS

There are prayers for victory in every area of your life!

After reading and translating books on prayer, there is a common pattern I noticed that secures victory in every area of our lives—obedience. Though at times it might seem that God is tarrying and delaying answers to healing, breakthrough, or the desires of our hearts, God is always working. He is indeed the Waymaker, Miracle Worker, Light in the darkness, and works all things for your good as you love Him.

Pray these prayers throughout the day, every day:

*Father God, take over.*
*Father God, fight my battles.*
*Father God, thank You always.*
*Father God, guide me!*
*Father God, help me!*
*Father God, have mercy on me!*
*Father God, use me for Your purposes and glory!*
*Father, I worship You alone!*
*Father God, break off every generational curse and deliver me from all evil!*
*Father God, I surrender all and I trust You completely!*

The last prayer is the summary of the Lord's prayer in one phrase. Everything in the faith life begins with surrender, continues with endurance, and victory is secured through obedience. Whenever Israel obeyed God, they defeated their enemies and conquered Canaan, all the way to the Promised Land.

If there is any sin or guilt in your heart, repent to God and let no hidden sins remain. Live a life of obedience, and that will start giving you more and more victory and breakthrough in every area of your life. Whether faith, finance, family, friendships, health, or ministry concerns, prayer changes the impossible to possible and is the lifeline of the Christian. Be sure of your salvation as you work out your salvation with fear and trembling. (See Philippians 2:12.) There is then no fear of going to hell, or being half-certain of your salvation.

God bless us all to live the Spirit-filled and biblical Christian Life as we have more and more testimonies of Jesus' grace and goodness and love in our lives! We prove to ourselves, God, and our conscience, that we are indeed people going to Heaven when we live lives worthy of the Gospel and His blood.

> *Worthy is the Lamb who was slain, to receive power and riches and wisdom, and strength and honor and glory and blessing!* (Revelation 5:12 NKJV)

# 12

# ASSURANCE OF SALVATION

## HOW SHALL WE REPENT?

Those who truly repent and live lives worthy of Jesus' death on the Cross can go to Heaven. It is not our job to judge who goes to Heaven or hell, for only God is the Judge of all living and dead. However, we see biblical examples, characters, and modern-day people, both famous and hidden, who truly live godly lives and are sure of going to Heaven after death.

As we live the church life, it is possible to gradually discover the way to true faith. It is not useless to have church life classes for new believers at times. As a principle, the new believer should learn how to truly repent, surrender to Jesus, and walk the Christian life first, before taking classes on church life. This is where the issue of "how should we believe" emerges.

> *This is a faithful saying and worthy of all acceptance, that Christ Jesus came into the world to save sinners, of whom I am chief* (1 Timothy 1:15 NKJV).

These words of Paul teach us the way one who truly repented, views oneself, as a sinner in need of a Savior, the Savior. It is interesting that the first step in escaping hell where sinners go, is to recognize we are sinners. Then we can know why Jesus Christ came to earth, to save!

Understanding the main purpose of why Jesus came to earth and our identity in Him is crucial to living an effective Christian life. Our faith is directly tied to how deeply we grasp the truth that Jesus came to save sinners, and what that means for our identity in Him. We cannot afford to see Jesus through the lens of traditional religions, nor as just a revolutionary or philosopher. Some may refer to Him casually as a king or a leader of a peaceful movement, but as believers, we cannot settle for such views.

Jesus came solely to save sinners. If the sin problem is not dealt with first, nothing else truly matters in life. Societal reformation, improvements in systems, and other attempts to make things better will always fall short if the root issue of sin is not resolved. When we truly understand why Jesus came to earth, we realize that sinners are the ones who need Him the most.

With that in mind, the question *"How should we repent and believe in Jesus?"* becomes essential.

## FIRST: RECOGNIZE WE ARE INDEED SINNERS

The story of Cain and Abel and the first sacrifices offered to God illustrates this truth of recognizing our sinfulness. Cain didn't acknowledge his own sinfulness when he brought his offering to God, and therefore, God didn't accept it. On the other hand, Abel understood he was a sinner and knew that he couldn't approach God without a blood offering. That's why he prepared a lamb to offer to God—because God had already revealed this way of atonement to Adam and Eve.

This truth remains unchanged today. The only way to come before God is through the blood. Whether in Abel's time or ours, we walk by faith before God only through the blood of Jesus, but first, we must recognize that we are sinners. God Himself provided this way, but it's only for those who acknowledge their sin.

## SECOND: DISCOVER OUR SINS

Being aware of our sin is not enough. The Bible says, "*. . . To those who eagerly wait for Him He will appear a second time, apart from sin, for salvation*" (Hebrews 9:28 NKJV). As believers, waiting on Jesus is our primary duty, but there's more: we must be *"apart from sin"* when He returns. This means we must continually discover and crucify our sins before His second coming.

To truly believe in Jesus is to recognize and confront our sins. This doesn't mean the work of salvation—Jesus completed that on the Cross when He declared, *"It is finished!"* (John 19:30). But those who accept His forgiveness must also engage in the ongoing work of discovering their sins and crucifying them. This process of sanctification is an ongoing duty for believers.

We cannot treat the work of sanctification as if it's equal to the completed work of salvation on the Cross. The Cross was the ultimate act of redemption, but now, as followers of Jesus, we are called to fight against sin—*"to the point of shedding your blood"* (Hebrews 12:4 NIV). This is our responsibility as we live out the Christian life here on earth. Our role is to wait upon the Lord and actively participate in the work of faith.

The depth of our faith is directly connected to the depth of our awareness of our sinfulness. The more we identify our sin, the more we recognize our need for Jesus. When we stop actively searching our hearts and recognizing the areas where we fall short, our faith begins to wane. But when we are diligent in discovering our sins and bringing them to the Cross, our faith becomes stronger and deeper.

So how do we discover our sins? Are the sins we uncover simply bad habits, or do they go deeper to our souls, hearts, and even generational lineage? The process of truly discovering our sins is not about just acknowledging the surface-level wrongs. It is about digging deeper into our hearts, asking the Holy Spirit to reveal every hidden area where sin may be lingering, and bringing it before Jesus for forgiveness and transformation.

A certain level of sin awareness is not unique to believers—anyone can notice the wrongs that violate legal or societal rules. However, as Christians, we need to see our sins not with the eyes of the flesh, but with spiritual eyes, and through the eyes of our Lord Jesus, whose gaze is like fire. We might think we know all our sins when we look at them with our natural eyes, but those sins that we can write down or categorize with our fleshly perspective are not the real issue. The deeper, hidden sins, the ones we cannot see with our eyes or write on a list, are the ones that truly need to be dealt with.

The more we dive into this process, the more we realize just how deep our sin runs. Like Paul, we cry out, *"O wretched man that I am! Who will deliver me from this body of death?"* (Romans 7:24 NKJV). This is not a flippant statement—Paul truly understood the weight of his sin. Isaiah, too, cried out when he recognized his own unworthiness: *"Woe is me, for I am undone!"* (Isaiah 6:5 NKJV). These deep sighs and cries are signs that we are beginning to uncover the depths of our sin.

When we truly discover our sins, it often leads to a feeling of self-loathing. Job's story is a perfect example of this. At first, he was consumed with confusion and frustration, unable to understand why he was going through such extreme trials. Despite his victory over his friends' accusations, Job couldn't find peace because he couldn't reconcile his sinfulness. It was only when Job encountered God and saw His perfection that he came to understand his own brokenness. He said, *"I have heard of You by the hearing of the ear, but now my eye sees You. Therefore I abhor myself, and repent in dust and ashes"* (Job 42:5-6 NKJV).

When Job says, *"I abhor myself,"* he is not just acknowledging his mistakes, he's expressing a deep, personal detestation of his old nature. One of the key steps in truly repenting for real spiritual growth is realizing just how deeply broken we are, and this often leads to hating our old selves—our sinful nature. Jesus Himself says, *"If anyone desires to come after Me, let him deny himself, and take up his cross, and follow Me"* (Matthew 16:24 NKJV). To deny oneself is to detest our sinful nature, to set aside our own desires and self-interest in pursuit of Jesus.

So how should we repent and believe? We do so by denying and detesting our old selves. Job overcame his trials when he recognized that his real enemy was not his friends, nor his circumstances, but his own sinfulness. Despite his friends' attempts to correct him with legalistic and traditional arguments, they could not help him. Job's breakthrough came when he acknowledged his sin and repented before God. Only then did everything else begin to fall into place.

This process of discovering and detesting our sin is not just a mental exercise; it is a crucial step in living a life worthy of the Gospel. As we identify our sin, confess it, and allow God to work in us, we demonstrate to ourselves, to God, and to our consciences that we are indeed walking in the truth of His sacrifice. In this space is where we find grace and peace, and that our lives align with the redemptive power of Jesus' blood.

Ultimately, when we truly understand the depth of our sin and respond to it, we prove to ourselves that we are people destined for Heaven, living lives worthy of the Gospel and His blood.

## REPENT TO RECEIVE FORGIVENESS OF SIN

On the subject of why we must truly repent and believe in Jesus, as I have written beforehand, all people are sinners:

> *...For we have already made the charge that Jews and Gentiles alike are all under the power of sin* (Romans 3:9 NIV).

> *For all have sinned and fall short of the glory of God* (Romans 3:23 NKJV).

The biggest problem for all people is the issue of sin. Those who realize they are sinners have tried and strived to solve this problem. They invented many methods to try to resolve it. Let's listen to some of the more known ones, which in truth, *do not lead to Heaven.*

## SOME TRY TO RECEIVE FORGIVENESS THROUGH A LIFE OF SUFFERING.

Many people throughout history in various cultures have heard that the flesh commits sin, and therefore many have tried to destroy it by voluntarily inflicting suffering on their own bodies. I also see that overall, people in the East are more into entering lives of suffering than people in the West. When one speaks of religion, we see many trying to live lives of suffering through living lives of isolation, renunciation, and voluntary poverty.

Denying the desires of the flesh is another popular way people tried to overcome sin. There are some benefits to denying our eating or sexual desires, but how can we overcome sin when sin begins in the heart, not the body? Jesus correctly taught that whoever covets already committed the sin of robbery, and those who lust with their eyes already committed adultery.

Maybe people can endure such self-denial to train themselves to achieve their resolute dreams, but they cannot deny their flesh to change the sins already committed. In pagan religions, people think living the life of suffering might pay for their sins, and thereby leave their homes, deny themselves sleep, food, live naked and wretched, or even live as beggars—but these attempts to receive forgiveness for sin are all just a complete waste of time. If it is to train the body such behavior can be beneficial, but if it is to solve the problem of sin, such methods are futile and foolish.

## SOME TRY TO RECEIVE FORGIVENESS BY STORING UP GOOD DEEDS.

There are many who try to resolve the problem of sin by stacking up good deeds and works. In some religions, for example, its followers boast and claim that they have never murdered anyone, but they may also observe certain customs, such as releasing fish they have caught on specific days to receive forgiveness of sins from a god. While these acts may be cultural or symbolic, they do not address the root issue of sin. Good deeds and rituals like these don't resolve our problem of sin or pay for our sins.

I once observed a religious holiday in China, a big event in rural towns where people were rushing around celebrating. There were merchants everywhere selling fish—huge fish such as wild and domestic carp. I watched for a while, and what I saw will stay with me. A wealthy woman came up, repeating congratulatory words to herself, bought a large fish at a hefty price, and released it into the shallow waters of a nearby pond. As soon as she turned to walk away, the merchant scooped the fish back out of the water and began selling it again to another person. This happened repeatedly, over and over. The merchants were profiting from this, making money off a ritual that didn't solve anything.

This kind of self-satisfying, superficial good deed is meaningless. Will such actions really pay for our sins? Of course not. It is a waste of time and only serves to deceive ourselves. These rituals, no matter how meaningful or spiritual they may feel in the moment, do nothing to address the true problem of sin, which is within.

## SOME TRY TO RECEIVE FORGIVENESS BY PAYING FOR SINS WITH INDULGENCES OR RANSOM MONEY.

Around the world, many cultures practice the idea of paying for sins through indulgences or ransom money. We cannot deny that some have even attempted this within Christianity, but it's a complete misrepresentation of the Gospel. Peter, in Acts 8:20 (NIV), condemned such practices when he said to Simon the sorcerer, *"May your money perish with you."* The idea that we can buy forgiveness with money is not only misguided—it's blasphemous. Those who think they can pay for forgiveness with money are, as Paul says, people whose god is their appetite (Philippians 3:19).

Rather than resolving the issue of sin, paying indulgences only leads people into more sin. And the more we see these practices across different cultures and religions, the clearer it becomes that many have bought into superstitions without understanding their origins or true meaning.

## HOW TO REALLY REPENT AND RECEIVE THE FORGIVENESS OF SINS

Now the truth is, there is only one way to truly deal with our sins, and it's not through good works, rituals, or payment—it's through "substitutionary atonement." God, in His unchanging righteousness, has already determined that *"the wages of sin is death"* (Romans 6:23). That is the unalterable, spiritual reality. No amount of good deeds or rituals can change the fact that sin demands death.

Regardless, in His great love, God Himself provided the way for us. The only path to life was for God to become man—Jesus Christ came to pay for our sins, offering Himself as the perfect, sinless substitute. This is the Gospel. This is the meaning and the power of the Cross of Jesus Christ.

Through Jesus' incarnation, God took on the penalty of sin that should have been ours. His death on the Cross was the only way to satisfy the righteous requirements of God's law, while also demonstrating

His love for us. As Romans 5:8 (NKJV) says, *"But God demonstrates His own love toward us, in that while we were still sinners, Christ died for us."*

This is the truth of substitutionary atonement: Jesus paid the price for us, and there's nothing left for us to pay. His life and death fulfilled the demands of God's law, and it was not just a theoretical concept or philosophy—it was the reality of His life, His sacrifice. This is the only and complete way to solve the problem of sin. It is the ultimate expression of God's love and His desire to save us.

Through the Cross, God has provided the only way to truly be forgiven and reconciled to Him. Nothing else will ever suffice.

True repentance means fully believing in and trusting Jesus' atoning work on the Cross for your and my sins. At the heart of it, our basic and ultimate duty as humans is to believe in the life and sacrifice of our Lord Jesus Christ. When we believe that Jesus has completely paid for all our sins and demonstrated His incredible love for us, we receive the forgiveness of our sins. However, if we do not believe this truth and reject it, even though Jesus died for our sins, we will not be able to experience the power of that forgiveness, nor will we avoid hell.

There is no human-made method that can pay for our sin. Iti s not about striving or working harder. It's about believing that Jesus finished the work, that our sins are fully paid for and forgiven through His sacrifice. This is the heart of Christianity. To believe this is to truly live the Christian life—and part of that life is sharing these truths with others.

This is how we solve humanity's most egregious problem, the problem of sin. Throughout history and across cultures, people have tried countless methods to deal with sin, but in the end, the answer was not found in human effort—the answer is found completely in God alone. And this is why Christians can sing the song of ultimate victory, because Jesus has already done it all!

## CAN AN EASYGOING, WORLDLY LIFE FILLED WITH WICKEDNESS AND LAZINESS LEAD SOMEONE TO HELL?

In 2 Corinthians 6:9-10 (NKJV), Paul says, "*As unknown, and yet well known; as dying, and behold we live; as chastened, and not yet killed; as sorrowful, yet always rejoicing; as poor, yet making many rich; as having nothing, and yet possessing all things.*" These verses help us understand two ways of living: the dark side and the bright side.

Some people live life constantly crying, finding every excuse to complain, resent, and live in anxiety. Others live with a smile, optimistic, and unfamiliar with worry or fear. The former is living on the dark side, while the latter is living on the bright side of life.

Sadly, we see too many stories about the dark side in the media these days. Some young people, driven by immaturity or rebellion, get involved in foolish and dangerous activities—including committing crimes or seeking attention in destructive ways. It's hard to understand why the media keeps giving these dark stories so much attention, almost as if they're promoting a twisted sense of heroism. If the media chose to focus on positive, uplifting stories, society would be better off.

Even in our personal lives, imagine if we shared only the bright side with others—our smiles, optimism, and kind words. How much more uplifting would that be? Instead, when we show our sadness, anger, or frustration, it only spreads negativity, anxiety, and resentment. Laughter and joy can lift us up, while sorrow and negativity drag us down.

Paul's words about being "*unknown and yet well known*" remind us that living humbly, without trying to promote ourselves or chase fame, brings peace. People who seek fame often experience anxiety and frustration. But those who humbly serve, who may hide themselves in service to others, eventually find their true worth revealed in God's timing. They become well known in the best way.

The next line, *"as dying, and behold we live,"* speaks to the reality that living a truly fulfilled life isn't about striving endlessly to better ourselves at the expense of others. The true power to live a good life is given from above. When people selfishly make life hell for others to gain something for themselves, they are heading toward destruction. But those who live selflessly, sacrificing for others, will find that they gain life, not death. Sacrifice may feel like a loss, but it leads to a richer, fuller life, one that doesn't end in despair.

Paul says, *"as sorrowful, yet always rejoicing."* Even in the face of hardship, the joy of the Lord remains at the center. It's not about worrying over basic needs, status, or comforts. For the apostle Paul, his sorrow was for the souls he wanted to reach and for the Church he loved. His anxiety wasn't about personal survival but about the spiritual well-being of others. And despite the difficulties, he found joy and comfort in the Lord's love and grace.

Living a life that focuses on others, full of self-sacrifice and joy in the face of challenges, may seem like a difficult path, but it's the path to real peace and fulfillment. And, more importantly, it's the path that leads to life—eternal life in Christ.

*"As poor, yet making many rich"*—in the world's eyes, poverty is often associated with a lack of money, status, or fame. However, there is a distinction between material poverty, spiritual poverty, and religious poverty. Material poverty cannot make someone else materially rich, but when it comes to faith, it is a whole different story. You can be poor in material things but still have a rich, thriving faith life. The Bible even tells us that it is easier for a camel to pass through the eye of a needle than for a rich man to enter Heaven (Matthew 19:24).

Material wealth does not translate to spiritual wealth. Material poverty can open the door to spiritual riches. Money has wings, it is an illusion, and Paul says with food and clothing we shall be content (1 Timothy 6:8), and that:

> *Those who desire to be rich fall into temptation, into a snare, into many senseless and harmful desires that plunge people into ruin and destruction. For the love of money is a root of all kinds of evils. It is through this craving that some have wandered away from the faith and pierced themselves with many pangs* (1 Timothy 6:9-10 ESV).

Money is overrated, and we cannot take even a penny to Heaven with us. If you have it, share it. If you do not, work harder to feed your family, and God will guide you when you work faithfully and with gratitude. All in all, which kind of wealth do you really desire?

Take Peter and John, for example. When they came across a beggar at the temple gate, they said, "Silver and gold we do not have." Yet, they had something far more precious to offer: the name of Jesus Christ. Their material poverty did not hold them back. They gave what they had, and through their faith in Jesus, that beggar was made rich, whole, and healthy, things money could not buy. Peter and John had no money to give, but they gave the life-changing name of Jesus, which was more valuable than gold. They did not just enrich one beggar, they enriched many lives. Having Jesus meant greater wealth than anything the world could offer.

*"As having nothing, and yet possessing all things"*—these are Paul's last words in 2 Corinthians 6:9-10 and they show us the truth about the supremacy of Christ. Paul, once a man of status and wealth, counted everything as loss for the sake of knowing Christ. He considered all his previous accomplishments as rubbish in comparison to the surpassing worth of Christ (Philippians 3:7-8). When you have Jesus, you realize that all things belong to you. Everything else pales in comparison to the treasure of knowing Christ.

## WITH JESUS, ALL IS YOURS

This points to the central truth of the Christian life: when you have Jesus, you truly have everything. You can give up everything else, knowing that in Christ, all things are yours. This is the key to living a leisurely life, a life of peace. The reason we often live stressed, rushed, and irritated is because we don't have the Lord fully in the center of our lives. When we make Him our everything, it changes everything. With the Lord in our lives, we can live with peace and a smile, no matter the circumstances.

As missionary Heidi Baker in Mozambique, whose team raised 120 people from the dead and feeds thousands of orphans daily in one of the most persecuted regions in the world against Christianity, says, "There is always enough." There is always enough to go around for everyone, when we have Jesus. There is no lack. If you meet someone who is crying or struggling, it is often because they are lacking something. They are missing the one thing that can always, truly satisfy—the Lord Jesus. Those who know Jesus never lack.

As Psalm 23 says, *"The Lord is my shepherd; I shall not want."* We are not lacking because we do not have enough money or material things. If we are crying, it is because we are missing the Lord. Without Him, we are always poor.

This truth applies even in our service to the Lord. Those who serve poorly often do so because they are spiritually poor. They are rushing through their service, distracted and lacking the peace that comes from truly being with the Lord. When we serve with the Lord at the center of our lives, our service becomes full, joyful, and even pleasant. We do not rush or feel pressed for time. Rather, we serve with deep, abiding peace.

Let us live with that kind of commitment to serving the Lord, fully surrendered, and fully present. In doing so, we will find comfort, peace, and joy, no matter what life throws our way.

# 13

# STORING UP TREASURES IN HEAVEN

I was preaching another revival on a Sunday with a church in Texas, via zoom. It was a predominantly a South Indian immigrant church. This Pentecostal church asked me to share on seeing hell, Heaven, repentance, and how to evangelize as a church.

Evangelism is both taught and caught. As we deny ourselves and go out to save souls daily and weekly, we become addicted to holy habits. It becomes a whole other level, because Jesus is the Most High. After tasting Him, there is no need to go back to a substitute. Once you get spiritually and naturally high on Him, you need nothing else. You will be addicted to Him.

Your food becomes Jesus food. What exactly is Jesus food? What did He eat on earth to walk as the Son of God that we too may imitate Him?

> *Meanwhile the disciples were urging him, saying, "Rabbi, eat." But he said to them, "I have food to eat that you do not know about." So the disciples said to one another, "Has anyone brought him something to eat?" Jesus said to them,* ***"My food is to do the will of him who sent me and to accomplish his work****"* (John 4:31-34 ESV).

Then the disciples asked Jesus, what is His work or will? Jesus explains this in John 6:39-40 (ESV):

> *And this is the will of him who sent me, that I should lose nothing of all that he has given me, but raise it up on the last day. For this*

> *is the will of my Father, that everyone who looks on the Son and believes in him should have eternal life, and I will raise him up on the last day.*

Again, it is about saving souls, sharing the Gospel. To store up treasures in Heaven, we must save souls. "Empty hell, populate Heaven" are not just words on a Christian t-shirt, they proclaim the very will of our Father in Heaven! It the King of king's mandate for us. To abide in God's love—the desire of every Christian and person once they know how good and wonderful He is—we must obey His commandments. His commandments are not burdensome, they are given to us to love Him and to love our neighbors as ourselves.

Who are our neighbors? Everyone and anyone around us. To abide in His love, we have to love people, all types of people: rich, poor, big, small, old, young, every color and class. You get the point. And when we love our neighbors, we share the Gospel with them. To abide in God's love and to eat Jesus' food, which truly satisfies every desire in our hearts, we must worship God, for we were created to worship, and save souls—evangelize!

How do we evangelize? Whenever we can, however we can, wherever we can, by all means we can, to whomever we can, is how we evangelize.

We can have trances, dreams, visions, and even encounters with God. These will all lead us to evangelize when we truly understand God's heart. Jesus is the Shepherd who will leave the 99 to save the one lost sheep. "The Church is a gas station, not a destination," are the words of Pastor Vlad Savchuk of HungryGen, because many lost souls are outside the four walls of the Church. See Jesus' words after His resurrection and He was ascending:

> *Afterward he appeared to the eleven themselves as they were reclining at table, and he rebuked them for their unbelief and hardness of heart, because they had not believed those who saw*

> *him after he had risen. And he said to them, "**Go into all the world and proclaim the gospel** to the whole creation. **Whoever believes and is baptized will be saved**, but whoever does not believe will be condemned"* (Mark 16:14-16 ESV).

Glory to God. Hallelujah! It is the year and season of the evangelist. Evangelism is happening all around the globe in the body of Christ. Many Christians and churches are waking up, going out beyond the four church walls to proclaim the Gospel to all creation. He is also calling you to share God's love, so that all those around you do not have to spend eternity in hell.

Now is the day of salvation. Today is a time of grace. That is our mindset daily for revival and evangelism. When we fix our hearts on the finished work of the Cross, we evangelize because we are saved, not to be saved. Charles Spurgeon, the prince of preachers, told his listeners this now-famous quote: "Have you no wish for others to be saved? Then you're not saved yourself, be sure of that!"

Tell yourself and pray and proclaim, "I am going to save 100 souls this year!" Tell your church friends, pastors, and yourself, *I am going to be leading at least 100 souls to Christ this year.* And we have God's grace and Spirit to help us. We are simply joining His work and mission, not starting our own movement or mission. It is His mission, also called the Great Commission, and as such, we are not to worry about the results, but to go forward, for God desires all people to be saved more than we do.

My testimony became a documentary movie titled, *After Death,* and the well-established Christian media Angel Studios picked it up. It is not just my story, but a group of stories of people who all had near-death experiences, saw Heaven, hell, or both, and met Jesus Christ to become new creations. The movie can be found in every major streaming medium, except Netflix, and became the number-one selling documentary in the history of the United States. In the whole history of the US. It grossed tens of millions of dollars. And I got a burrito for payment. Hallelujah! I am so grateful because here on earth, with food and clothing, we shall be content. My rewards that last are in Heaven.

> *And having food and clothing, with these we shall be content* (1 Timothy 6:8 NKJV).

Pleasing Jesus is my motivation. I am so joyful when I please my Lord, God, and Savior. He is also my best friend, in the sense that I trust Him and am here to be with Him, more than anyone else or any other created thing. Therefore, I signed a form saying, take it all, media companies, my rewards are in Heaven. Theirs is too, as long as they have the same attitude. We cannot serve both God and money. We use money to save souls. We provide for our families, but there is no room for greed in the Kingdom of God.

I was born into a Buddhist home—my mother and father met at a temple as part of an arranged marriage and they were married in the temple. I was born in the temple and was dedicated to the service of Buddha.

After accepting Jesus as my personal Savior, I realized why I experienced so much depression and why my life was so messed up. Talk about birthrights. God hates idolatry and if you have been involved in other religions or worshiped other gods beside the God of Heaven, Father of Jesus Christ, the Holy Spirit, please renounce your past and repent. There is none of that death and depression with Christ. He fights your battles as you store up treasures in Heaven. There is no better deal or lifestyle than to live for Jesus here on earth. Nothing compares!

I was in the Buddhist temples seeking eternal life, seeking the purpose of life from the age of 6. While other kids were watching cartoons, I was asking questions like, "Why was I born? Why is that guy richer than me? How come he is better off than me? Why is there suffering in life? What is the purpose of life? How do I escape all this pain hidden within me?" The Buddhist monks told me, "If you pray, Steve, pray for a million years, get reincarnated 100 times, maybe you can become a Buddha." They call it reaching nirvana, or enlightenment.

I asked, "When do I start?"

They answered me, "You should start now."

I replied, "You are right. A million years is a long time. I should and must start now." Therefore, I was striving, praying to Buddha eight hours a day. Even in high school, before going to class, in the USA and more so in Korea. I got up early almost every morning trying to get this Buddha to talk to me and for me to reach nirvana. He never talked to me or winked at me or acknowledged me. It was a one way, unbalanced relationship, very unhealthy.

However, do you know that only our living God talks? Our Jesus Christ, Almighty Savior, talks because He is alive. He is well. He talked to me this morning. We are in His spiritual presence. He is God. He loves you. He is Spirit, but we too are spiritual beings for we are made in His image.

> *He who planted the ear, does he not hear? He who formed the eye, does he not see? He who disciplines the nations, does he not rebuke? He who teaches man knowledge—the Lord—knows the thoughts of man, that they are but a breath* (Psalm 94:9-11 ESV).

Before personally meeting and encountering Jesus Christ, I did not know any of this about God. I never read one verse in the Bible. I was in the temples every weekend. I grew up in a very Buddhist home. I actually came to America seeking the American dream. My father was a wealthy businessman at the time. He did not even know how to drive a car—he had drivers who drove the car for him. He made a lot of money, and I thought to myself, *I will become an attorney and make money for myself, feed myself, live for myself.*

Let us see what Jesus says about those who live for themselves, and not for God:

> *And he told them a parable, saying, "The land of a rich man produced plentifully, and he thought to himself, 'What shall I do, for I have nowhere to store my crops?' And he said, 'I will do this: I will tear down my barns and build larger ones, and there I will store all my grain and my goods. And I will say to my soul, "Soul, you have ample goods laid up for many years; relax, eat, drink, be merry."' But God said to him, 'Fool! This night your soul is required of you, and the things you have prepared, whose will they be?' So is the one who lays up treasure for himself and is not rich toward God"* (Luke 12:16-21 ESV).

If I knew Jesus was the Lord, I would have never lived for myself. My only regret in life is that I was not saved in high school. I would have told all my friends at the high schools in Boston and Seoul that Jesus is Lord! Surrender all to Him! It is a better, far superior life.

How do we store up treasures in Heaven? By carrying out His will! What is His will? That we save souls.

As mentioned previously, if you want to make God laugh, there is only one thing you need to do. Tell Him your life plans and goals, without consulting Him. That is what I did before meeting Him. I had my whole life planned out. I drew the blueprints for the house I was going to live in. I was going to become an attorney, make lots of money, get married, have kids, have two dogs, three cars, and then die. I would have ended up forever in hell living for myself only.

It is not our religious label, how moral we look in front of others in society, or how holy we look at church that matters. We must live according to God's will to go to Heaven. That is the sign that we truly know Him personally, and that our faith is real. We are not saved by works, but they prove that you received real grace. Jesus, nonetheless, says do not fear. He says honor and trust Him completely, and He will bring you safely home.

> *I tell you, my friends, do not fear those who kill the body, and after that have nothing more that they can do. But I will warn you whom to fear: fear him who, after he has killed, has authority to cast into hell. Yes, I tell you, fear him! Are not five sparrows sold for two pennies? And not one of them is forgotten before God. Why, even the hairs of your head are all numbered. Fear not; you are of more value than many sparrows* (Luke 12:4-7 ESV).

During my near-death experience in 1998, I experienced firsthand the judgment of God, and then His mercy. As mentioned in Chapter 2, when I smoked what in the street is called the deathbowl, filled with heroin, cocaine, and PCP, I stayed awake for 10 straight days. Fentanyl kills about 50,000 to 60,000 people a year in the US. Back in those days, it was heroin that killed most people from drugs. I was not just hallucinating at the time, but I felt very anxious.

Nowadays, Gen Z and young people whom I meet and minister to tell me about their anxiety attacks, even without doing drugs. Every time we pray in Jesus' name, I see them healed. Are there rewards to ministry? According to apostles Paul and John in the New Testament, yes there is. However, the greatest reward is pleasing Jesus, bringing people into Heaven, and seeing them together in eternity.

By the fifth day of my ordeal, I didn't know what time of the day it was. By the sixth and seventh day, when I looked in the mirror I saw that my pupils were so big and black. The white parts of my eyes were hardly visible. I felt and knew I was going to die soon. I felt extremely restless, anxious, depressed, fearful for 240 hours. In other words, I believe I was demon possessed. I didn't know spiritual warfare was real—but I did know I was losing a life-threatening battle.

I still attended classes, but when the teachers and my friends were talking to me, I could not process even a sentence of what they were saying. I kept asking myself, *Where am I? What class am I in?* I opened the textbook and turned to page so and so. I literally looked at the pages of the book but could not read even one sentence. This is when the devil came to me, disguised as an angel of light himself.

I feel the need to repeat some of what you read in Chapter 2 as the experience is so overwhelmingly frightful that I pray it keeps even one soul from going to hell. The devil spoke to me saying, "If you kill yourself, offer your body as a sacrifice to me. I will give you 50,000 less years in hell." What a liar the devil is. Only God can send someone to Heaven or hell, as we just read in Luke chapter 12. However, it sounded like a good deal at the time, because I didn't have Jesus Christ in my life. I wrote a letter to my mom, my poor and broken-hearted mother. In the letter, I summarized my failures in life, apologized for not making her proud, and that I hoped to see her in the afterlife.

As she read the letter, she started to sob and cry. I said, "Mom, I'm sorry that I failed you in life. I am so sorry I failed you in life. I love you so much, but I don't know what else to do. There is nothing I can do…."

## DAY 10

On day 10, around September 11, 1998, I went to the kitchen and I grabbed the biggest knife I could find, and I got on my knees. I had no idea how to commit suicide. I had never cut or stabbed myself before. I was very scared. However, trying to escape hell with my own understanding, I put the knife to my stomach and then my neck. My poor mom saw me in this position from the hallway.

She called 911; we were living in Irvine at the time. Some say, Irvine has more police than civilians. It is a very safe city, at least in the natural. They arrived very quickly, within a few minutes. Four police officers with batons and mace showed up and commanded, "Put the knife down!"

The devil spoke to me again. The Asian grandpa said, "It is either now or never. Go for it! If you do not come to me now, you are going to have 50,000 more years in hell." I immediately cut my neck open, stabbing it as hard as I could multiple times, and did the same to my stomach. Blood was flowing everywhere in that small living room. The furniture broke as the policemen jumped toward me to restrain me from further injury. They hit me with their batons and then sprayed me with mace. I pray in Jesus' name that nobody reading this book gets maced—it's very painful. When they maced me, I dropped the knife and fell unconscious.

By this time, I had already cut parts of my arteries in my neck. I also punctured many parts of my body in the stomach area. My mother, and younger brother who came home later in that day, recall that the entire living room was covered with my blood. As I dropped the knife, the officers and paramedics picked me up and placed me on a stretcher. I was being transferred to the UC Irvine Medical Center, the emergency surgery center. I continued to fade in and out of consciousness and had what is called an out-of-body experience (OBE).

Leading up to this event, I called the Buddhist monks who had been discipling me, mentoring me my whole life. I made the very expensive international phone call from the US to Korea, requesting help. I shared with them that I felt I was under intense spiritual attack. Their response? Just like Buddha himself, eyes closed, stomach bloated out, "We are in the middle of a silent prayer. We cannot help you." I was so upset, disappointed, and frustrated. My mom was more than disappointed.

## FREE-FALLING INTO HELL

As for me, from the stretcher to the emergency room, while going in and out of consciousness, I was out of my body. I did not go upward toward Heaven. I did not see the Asian Grandpa anymore. He was nowhere in sight. Rather, I began to sink and sink. It was like a free-falling roller-coaster ride. The ride in Guardians of the Galaxy in Disneyland is good close comparison. However, unlike in that ride, I did not go back up, up, up. It was just went down, down, down.

After about what felt like five minutes of falling, I landed, *boom!* I looked around. You got to understand this. In Buddhism, there is no original sin. They do not believe in an eternal Heaven or hell. A person continues to be reincarnated. However, here I was, in Hell.

I was not alone. There were countless people in front of me, to my right, to my left, behind, with no end in sight. There were people's souls everywhere, as far as I could see in the dark. There was no sunlight. No plants. Just darkness, dirt, rocks, and reddish purplish colored cliffs. Gigantic demons wearing capes glared at me at and the souls surrounding me. Rather, I knew these creatures were gods in this place.

For the first time in my life, I knew a spiritual truth, or two spiritual truths rather. I instantly and supernaturally knew that I was a sinner, that I deserved to be there, and that I would never leave this place of eternal torment. Is that crazy or what?

In Buddhism, there is no concept of original sin or the need to repent. While on earth, I was the nicest Korean-America kid. I never hurt anyone. I never killed anyone. I sold drugs, but not the real bad ones. I sold only marijuana a few times. In my eyes, I was good enough to go to Heaven.

I thought to myself while alive, *My sins are not bad as Hitler's or Kim Jong Un's of North Korea.* However in God's eyes, a sinner is a sinner, and all fall short of going to Heaven without Jesus. Amen. There are only two types of people in this world: those who are born again and those who are not. I was definitely not born again at the time.

The emotional, physical, spiritual, relational—whatever adverb you can think of—pain that I felt on earth, was multiplied a hundredfold in hell. It was more painful in my heart, in my emotions, in my existence, in my being than anything I ever experienced. In hell, there is not even an inkling or a perception of God. It is a place God created to trap the devil, to judge him, and is void of God.

Anyone whose name is not written in the book of life, not born-again, or surrendered to Jesus, end up there because all people rightly deserve to be there. There I was in hell, as a statistic, standing there without hope.

The agony and the pain that I felt at that moment is something that no human being should feel. No human being should feel that separation from God. We were not created for hell, yet people choose to go there. So there I was, hopeless, helpless in hell.

## PRAISE GOD FOR PRAYER WARRIORS

Praise God for my mom! In her desperation at the emergency room while waiting for the results of my surgery, she called out to every god in the whole world. She later shared with me that she called on Allah, Buddha, Muhammad, Confucius, Yin-Yang, Taoist gods, Shinto gods, every name she could think of at the time. Then she remembered that her friend in California, Mrs. Kim, was a Christian. And she called her. She was the only friend she had at the time as an immigrant, new to Southern California.

Mrs. Kim, the mother of the friend that let me stay in the house as we were selling drugs together, was actually praying for me to get saved and that God would use me to proclaim the Gospel to her son and all his friends. Believe it or not, they were already going to church at the time, but not really saved. There are churchgoers who are not going to make it to Heaven, unless they repent.

God answered that prayer. My mom called her and asked Mrs. Kim in desperation, "What do I do?"

She replied, "This is spiritual warfare."

My mom says, "Spiritual what?"

"Spiritual warfare. We need to pray. Let me call the pastors and prayer warriors from Grace Ministries International. We'll start praying right away."

Unlike the monks, these loving Christians came rushing to the emergency room. Man did they pray. For eight hours they prayed for me, which was the duration of my surgery and coma. During my out-of-body experience, in hell, they were praying for me.

The vein surgeon specialist arrived at the right time and repaired the torn arteries and blood vessels. At first he told my mom, "I'm sorry, but the first surgery did not go successfully. Your son's blood pressure, heart rate, keeps dropping. Mrs. Kang, he might not make it. I think you might need to get ready to let him go." Imagine if the prayer warriors did not pray, and Jesus did not come.

After two surgeries, I regained consciousness, healed. Praise Jesus for intercessors. Afterward, the doctor said it was a miracle that I awakened, healed. Right before I opened my eyes, I did not see Jesus. However, I heard His voice. Jesus spoke to my spirit, "No more Buddhism, no more drugs, and I love you." I opened my eyes and thought, *Who was that speaking to me?*

When I opened my eyes, I noticed that my bed was surrounded by the prayer warriors. One of the older ladies looked at me and said, "In Jesus' name, devil be gone!" I replied softly from fatigue, "I am not the devil." Since I tried to kill myself half a day ago, maybe they did not want me jumping on them, as some do in the *The Exorcist* movie. There were staples holding my skin together around my stomach and neck, and tubes going in and out everywhere. I must have looked scary.

Then they asked me, "Do you want to accept Christ as your Lord and Savior?" I told them briefly what I saw during my OBE and NDE, and they replied with gentle yet intense voices, "We think you might have seen hell. You saw hell, which is in the Bible."

I replied, "Yeah, I think so too. And I do not want to go back there ever again. None of you should go there either." They asked me if I wanted to pray the sinner's prayer. I followed them in praying the sinner's prayer that day.

That was my introduction to biblical Christianity in Christ Jesus. Hallelujah and glory to our Father God! God is good, all the time. What a timely Savior and Lord Jesus is! The Word of God says there is a great reward for saving souls. I believe these evangelists who led me to Jesus and prayed me out of hell have rewards awaiting them in Heaven. When you and I, too, pray and save souls by leading people to Jesus, and disciple them, there is a great reward. It is written in Daniel 12:2-3 (ESV):

> *And many of those who sleep in the dust of the earth shall awake, some to everlasting life, and some to shame and everlasting contempt. And those who are wise shall shine like the brightness of the sky above; and those who turn many to righteousness, like the stars forever and ever.*

Proverbs 11:30 (NIV) says, *"The fruit of the righteous is a tree of life, and who is wise saves lives."* Why? The one who wins souls or evangelizes, understands the heart of *"God our Savior, who wants all people to be saved and to come to the knowledge of the truth"* (1 Timothy 2:3-4 NIV).

The discipleship experience was not easy at Grace Ministries International, and I was at times even deceived into following Jesus. I believe God has a sense of humor. An assistant pastor there named Pastor Kim said to me, "Steve, every Christian prays three hours a day. They also read the Bible once a day. There are 1,189 chapters in the Bible, so you should read 40 chapters of the Bible every day." Therefore, when I first got saved, I started reading 30 to 40 chapters of the Bible a day. I went to morning prayer within a month of coming out of the hospital. Though I was sick, I was there.

I prayed, "Lord Jesus, I want to learn how to pray. Not as I did in Buddhism, but to You, Lord Jesus. I want to encounter You! When will You show Yourself?" After prayer, I looked at my watch, and only 5 minutes had passed. It was harder to prayer longer than in Buddhism, because I knew Jesus was listening and therefore I was more self-conscious and careful in what I prayed, instead of just repeating mindless chanting prayers.

After a month or two I learned to intercede—to pray for others. I looked behind and around me as my prayer times grew longer, and after an hour, the majority of the hundreds who attended the 5:30 a.m. morning service were gone. After two hours, some of the pastors were gone. I asked myself, *What happened to the three-hour rule?* However, I just stayed and prayed, "O God, do something. Meet me."

And God encountered me.

After another few months, I was baptized in the Holy Spirit. I had dreams of the rapture, the end times, Great Tribulation, earthquakes, saw the second coming or return of Jesus a few times—and more importantly, the Word of God became alive and is living in my heart.

> *So then faith comes by hearing, and hearing by the word of God* (Romans 10:17 NKJV).

When the Holy Spirit fell, I rolled on the floor in the worship room for a minute. It was after the 8 p.m. weekday evening service. I then grabbed my Bible, which felt like it was on fire, got up, and preached my first sermon by myself. "Repent! Believe in the Bible, sinners!" I was preaching and I did not yet fully understand what had just happened, but the Holy Spirit knew. He got hold of me. I was born again and baptized in the Holy Spirit.

When Moses met God at the age of 80, he had actually waited 40 years in the wilderness beforehand. Before being used by God, Paul was in Saudi Arabia for three years, biblical scholars claim, after meeting

Jesus. Everyone who is used by God goes through the toughest training in life. To have rewards in Heaven, we have to learn how to submit and surrender to God. In other words, suffering for Jesus and discipling from Jesus is good for us.

> *Not only that, but we rejoice in our sufferings, knowing that suffering produces endurance, and endurance produces character, and character produces hope, and hope does not put us to shame, because God's love has been poured into our hearts through the Holy Spirit who has been given to us* (Romans 5:3-5 ESV).

I became a youth pastor at the age of 24, in the year 2004. I had one church member when I started—one sister sitting in front of me, who had just come out of rehab. It seemed that she did not like my sermons. We did not have a nice building, or even a worship team. We had a CD player. I would press play, hoping she would sing along with me. She did not say amen when I asked her to say amen. Sometimes, it was the most awkward service ever. Two people in an office room, while the Korean-speaking adults were in the next room for worship. I prayed, *God, I did not get saved for this, Lord. I did not get saved to preach to one sister on Sundays who doesn't seem to be enjoying my sermons too much.*

Therefore, I got on my knees. We build our churches, lives, families, ministries, next generation, and the nations, on our knees. A few weeks later, she brought her boyfriend, and another came in, and others brought their friends. Young adults came, they brought their friends, and they in turn brought their friends. And the church grew to about 14 people. Eventually, about 50 percent of them went on to become pastors and church leaders, all the others joined the worship team. I later found out that the first sister also became a youth pastor in 2024. Hallelujah, Jesus! God answers our prayers, whether it is a day later, or in this case, 20 years later.

## SURRENDER ALL TO JESUS

I know God answers prayers. I completely trust in Him, no matter what I feel or go through. I give glory to God for becoming my everything. I pray daily, "Jesus, I love You more than money, fame, ministry, life, family, and pleasures. I surrender all today to You, Jesus."

However, from 2004 to 2013, I was still physically sick, had chronic insomnia, could not run or exercise normally, still traumatized by what I saw in hell, still under attack by the temptations that I had when I was a Buddhist, still stressed by trying to be successful in ministry. This did not last one year, two years, or five years. The Lord in his infinite wisdom, for some reason, allowed me to go through this for 10 years. For 10 years, I never slept one night normally.

Looking back, I was not yet delivered, though I believe I was saved. In other words, I was not the most effective Christian I could be, and therefore did not have as much treasure in Heaven as I could have. When under stress or sickness, it is hard to love others. So in 2013, I burned out. I lost 30 pounds. This is before I met my wife. This is before I came to the end of myself. Even after seeing Heaven, hell, and having a radical testimony, even while I was evangelizing, and doing all these Christian things, I burned out. On the inside, within me, the Kingdom of God and the word of Jesus did not fully take root.

I prayed, "Lord, what do I do now? Have You forsaken me? At the time, I only weighed 125-130 pounds, and I did not even have energy to get up from my chair. I had to lay on the couch all day, though I prayed 10 years ago, "God, I'm going to build the biggest church for You in the world. It is going to be on fire. And here I am on the couch." I called 911 so many times during this time from constant anxiety attacks and convulsions that 911 called me back and said, "We're going to sue you, Steve. You call us five times a day. The whole city needs us, not just you." I broke the record, they said, for calling

911 in a time period of a few months. They were not even prank calls. Every two to three hours, I would get a seizure from the stress and spirit of sickness.

My few Christian friends at time knew about it. We would be eating outside at a restaurant, for they had mercy on me and picked me up. When the panic attacks came, my heartbeat would jump up to 180 all of a sudden. They would ask me, "Is it coming, Steve?" I would answer, "Yes, it is coming soon." And I would just collapse at times in the middle of the restaurants. The psychiatrists and doctors put me on 20 medication prescriptions. The doctors told me that I would never be able to quit taking these pills. Xanax, Lithium Carbonate, and anti-depressants were pills I took a few times daily, and I carried them with me in a small blue bag everywhere I went.

I had nightmares during this season in 2013 to 2014. I had open-eye visions of demons' faces laughing at me, as I heard them audibly, and I was faithless, hopeless, and powerless. I was in a worse state than before I had met Jesus, to be frank. I prayed, "God, I think I'm done. I gave everything I got, and here I am. What a miserable end. Just take me home." Even my mom and dad said, "You have this testimony, Steve, but we think it might be time for you to go home."

Everyone around me was saying bye to me again. "See you in Heaven, if I make it." I was ready to die. Then Jesus visited me while I was in the hospital. This time, He did not visit me to pull me out of hell, but to ask me to surrender. During this whole time of intense sickness from burnout, He was always with me.

> *"...I will never leave you nor forsake you." So we can confidently say, "The Lord is my helper. I will not fear; what can man do to me?" Remember your leaders, those who spoke to you the word of God. Consider the outcome of their way of life, and imitate their faith. Jesus Christ is the same yesterday and today and forever* (Hebrews 13:5-8 ESV).

I felt the power of the Holy Spirit go through my body for a few hours. I was healed. I knew it in my spirit.

Are you discouraged, sick, or at the end of your own strength and plans? Now you are ready to get used by God, and store up treasures in Heaven!

Then the church plants and ministries began to take off, when Jesus wanted them to grow, and where we were ready to serve people purely, powerfully, and in love and holiness. Revive The Nations was birthed after this season of training, and dozens of ministers and newly saved evangelists have joined, and millions have heard my testimony for God's glory alone. We get messages every single day: Help me, pray for me.... The list goes on.

Do I want to now build a ministry? The answer is no. Now we want to build, disciple, serve, and empower others to follow Jesus, avoid hell, go to Heaven, and store up much treasure. We want to see those we run with, and minister to, and learn from, go to Heaven.

During the hardest season of my life, God sent me mentors who wanted to love on me and heal me, not use me to just build a ministry. That is not a bad goal in itself, but without love, it is impure, might not have an eternal impact or reward, for love is the greatest (see 1 Corinthians 13). A mentor who was a loving man of God, named Pastor Joseph Lee, came into my life and called me daily, invited me to his house church of 40 people (now it has thousands gathering in person and tens of thousands online weekly and monthly) to see God heal me. I did not miss a week, and prayed with him weekly, though I was very weak and having seizures.

God did heal me from that burnout. I got a fresh wind of health and life, not to mention faith, purer faith, than before this suffering season. God can use a rock, if He so desires, to praise Him and save others. However, we have been praying for this DNA of fervent prayer as it is very powerful, very powerful. When the Holy Spirit visited me the day

He healed me, I myself felt the negative effects of the medicine breaking off and out of me. I felt my stomach clear and my lungs enlarge, and I knew I was healed.

## GRATEFULLY BLESSED

In fact, I became so healthy that the following month I joined the US Army. I became a First Lieutenant as a Chaplain, after prayer, to prevent suicide and to save souls. I was grateful to live in this blessed country, and extremely grateful to be healthier again. I was the oldest officer who began, 35 years old, and direct commissioned.

I prayed before I went, "Are You sure You want me to go, Lord, and join the army, Lord?" God answered me clearly, "Yes. Comfort my people there and preach." Without hesitation, I went, and during the final interview, shared my testimony of the suicide attempt, seeing hell and Heaven, and the lieutenant colonels and one-star general answered, "You're in. Put on a uniform, and speak to the soldiers. Encourage them, and share life with them. Be available for them."

I said, "Yes sir," and saluted, hoping I did so with the right form, for I had never saluted as a soldier before. During my service from 2014 to 2016, many were delivered and saved by His grace alone, and I met some good friends who loved Jesus there. Though it was not an easy experience, God trained me there regarding service, teamwork, selflessness, being on time, not making excuses, and getting stuff done. Just do it. I actually believe it is good for every young man in today's society, to join the miliary.

Recently I moved to a city in Orange County, and I live on Lamplighter Street. The cross streets are Burning Bush and Revival. The Lord speaks to me even through street signs. When we live in revival, as lamplighters, after we had our encounter with God at our burning bush, we learn that we are to live for Heaven. We no longer have to worry about going to hell—we live for Heaven with our minds set on the pure things above.

How do we store up treasures in Heaven? Surrender daily to Jesus. Whatever you and I try to hold on to, we will lose. On the other hand, whatever we lay it at Jesus' feet will become His and ours to keep forever.

> *Do not lay up for yourselves treasures on earth, where moth and rust destroy and where thieves break in and steal; but lay up for yourselves treasures in heaven, where neither moth nor rust destroys and where thieves do not break in and steal. For* ***where your treasure is, there your heart will be also*** (Matthew 6:19-21 NKJV).

The book of Colossians teaches and equips us to have the right thoughts as we live here on earth:

> *If then you were raised with Christ, seek those things which are above, where Christ is, sitting at the right hand of God. Set your mind on things above, not on things on the earth. For you died, and your life is hidden with Christ in God. When Christ who is our life appears, then you also will appear with Him in glory. Therefore put to death your members which are on the earth: fornication, uncleanness, passion, evil desire, and covetousness, which is idolatry. Because of these things the wrath of God is coming upon the sons of disobedience, in which you yourselves once walked when you lived in them* (Colossians 3:1-7 NKJV).

When we set out to make a resolution and determination, today and now, to fix our eyes on Jesus and Heaven, revival comes. I went to the eastern United States for revival, and for revival I went to Oklahoma, Korea, Toronto, San Diego and San Francisco, Los Angeles, Cambodia, South Korea, Indonesia, Thailand, Mexico, and with my wife to Haiti and Guatemala—and the book of Acts revival was everywhere. When I was sent by God to hundreds of churches in many states and nations, I began to really notice that the pastors and churches who invited me to minister and preach were already on fire, if not more so, than I was for Jesus Christ.

When we did not have a platform or podium to preach during some weekdays, it did not matter. We have never seen so many people come to Jesus Christ in the evangelism field. I was so joyful. On Tuesday evenings, Wednesday evenings, Thursday evenings, Saturday afternoons, even after church on Sundays, we went out to preach the Gospel and share Jesus Christ. Other people, newly saved or those sick of playing church, came out to join, and many new teams began to form from small to mega churches. I equipped and shared as best as I could, through on-the-job training and equipping, how to save souls boldly, with wisdom, warmth, and love too, of course, as we operated in the power of the Holy Spirit.

As of writing this chapter, we are also on day 1,522 of daily morning prayer via Zoom, which happens every day from Monday to Friday, with Saturdays praying on our own. As we stayed faithful and grateful and faith-filled, Christians and pastors from persecuted nations somehow connected with us and started joining the Zoom call, some every day.

They do not get on the Zoom prayer call to share with me about playing church, or about the food they had, or post about their vacation spots on their Instagram accounts. They share with me prayer requests such as, "Pastor Steve, my church just burned down. My church members just got killed from the government soldiers in the jungles of Burma. I lost my home. Can you pray for us? We are staying strong and praise God still."

Pastors from India, Kenya, Nigeria, Uganda, Bangladesh, Bhutan, Nepal, and other persecuted nations join to pray. I do not recall exactly how they found our prayer call, but they did. Praise God for technology that can be used to connect and build His Kingdom. They come in with humility, purity, with tears, and brokenness. It purifies me, and everyone else on the call. The blood of the martyrs and suffering of the persecuted Christians will purify your mindset and faith somehow.

Jesus said in His first recorded sermon to a massive crowd, *"Blessed are the poor in spirit, for theirs is the kingdom of heaven. Blessed are those who mourn, for they shall be comforted"* (Matthew 5:3-4 NKJV).

Every church is to be a revival, sending, and missional center. It is not about how many attend, but how many we send! When a church or Christians become missional and evangelism focused, our lives start to gain God's attention, receive His anointing, and He begins to open the doors of the Gospel for us.

I do ministry full time, and also work full time. I attend business and network meetings. We live diligently and consider it a blessing to meet nonbelievers and non-Christians. Jesus speaks to us through the apostle Paul in the New Testament, "No work, no food."

> *For even when we were with you, we commanded you this:* ***If anyone will not work, neither shall he eat.*** *For we hear that there are some who walk among you in a disorderly manner, not working at all, but are busybodies. Now those who are such we command and exhort through our Lord Jesus Christ that they work in quietness and eat their own bread* (2 Thessalonians 3:10-12 NKJV).

William Carey, the father of modern missions, wrote a book titled, *An Enquiry into the Obligations of Christians to use Means for the Conversion of the Heathens.* It is a missionary manifesto that challenges the Church and Christians to use its financial resources to spread the Gospel. However, we do not just labor for food, we also go to work to share Jesus Christ, through our actions and hard effort.

Furthermore, money has more meaning now. We have it not to hoard it, worship it, nor find comfort in it—but to use it for evangelism and missions. Our work is not just work, separate from church, we work as worship. Our "work becomes His message," as my mentor Pastor Timothy Oh, founder of Kingdom Business Redeemers and a prayer warrior missionary, often says.

## 14

# THE GREAT COMMISSION—EVANGELIZE

If you or your church is not evangelizing, you and your church must begin to evangelize. Start small, but start now, somewhere, anywhere. It is not the great suggestion, but the Great Commission. Jesus cries for the lost and the hurting. Jesus wept (John 11:35). Sometimes I just sit and cry by myself. Other Christians and prayer warriors are crying too. I cry sometimes for the lost, and at times out of gratitude for what Jesus did for me. He catches our tears in a bottle, it says in the Bible (Psalm 56:8).

My mentor is discipling a thousand families as of now, and has planted 16 churches in Wall Street offices. CFOs of some of the biggest companies in the USA came to Jesus Christ. One sent an email to all his employees: "God loves you." 50,000 people read it. The Gospel is not just for within the church walls or even in the streets, the Gospel is also for the workplace, our workplace. My daily buzz is to see one less person in hell. Do not return home until you see one less person in hell today.

## THE YEAR OF THE EVANGELIST

Many churches announced publicly that 2024 is the year of the evangelist. Many other churches announcing publicly that 2025 is the year of the evangelist. Our church, Jesus Center, and our lead pastor, Daniel Park, announced that we are praying to see 1,000 souls come to

Jesus this year! We are going to need more seats. This is good news and something to celebrate: to see no increase in hell and Heaven more crowded. Amen. Your house is going to become a house of prayer, your business a place of love and discipleship. We are planting churches everywhere: in gyms, offices, Starbucks, high school campuses, online, offline, and in areas without churches. It is no longer time for business as usual.

We even started services and share the Gospel at UFC Gym and LA Fitness. Do you work out? We need energy and health to serve God, and the Bible says that your body is actually now the temple of God's Spirit (1 Corinthians 3:16). By God's grace, while we were planting a church in downtown Fullerton, dozens of newcomers came to Jesus as we preached the Gospel and Pastor Timothy Oh discipled us. Others saw my movie *After Death* and some of the 50-plus interviews I did on YouTube, and they came to our church.

We took the same people to the UFC Gym where I went a few times a week to hold Saturday night outreach and Sunday services. We prayed for hundreds of people and even the workers there for a few months, until we got kicked out due to some nonbelieving customers complaining.

At LA Fitness near my home and other locations, I spoke with someone new almost every week about Jesus and gathered a hundred or so numbers. Why? To text and call them about Jesus Christ. If a 45-year-old, bi-vocational pastor can do this, you can reach many more souls yourself at the gym for Jesus!

I started to say hello regularly and introduce myself to some of the managers and employees at the LA Fitness gym, and I began to pray for them as well. They invited me to their homes, I had lunch with some of them and began to share the Gospel and more about Jesus. Many I spoke to who were working out were Muslims. I love Muslims. Jesus loves Muslims very much. Where I live in Irvine, California, there are many Muslims. No, they are not terrorists, and many of them are open to living a better life and even to hearing about Jesus Christ.

One day at LA Fitness, I was working out wearing my Jesus shirt proudly and praying for divine appointments. I saw about 10 young, high school Muslim youths. They gathered in the middle of the gym, then laid out some rugs. I thought to myself, how bold of them, and interesting. They started bowing toward Mecca and practicing *salah*—praying five times a day, no matter where one may be at the time of prayer. Everyone in the gym stared at them.

As I worked out and minded my own business, something in my spirit was stirred up. I had the urge for them to meet the same Jesus I met. I got up from my bench and walked toward them, mainly because I felt so much love for them. I said, "Hello, brothers. How are you?" They got up from their rugs and replied, "Hello." When they got up, many of them were about 6 feet tall. I looked up to their faces and said, "Guys, Jesus loves you."

They replied, "Yeah, we know. But right now, we're doing our prayers. You're interrupting us."

I replied, "Excuse me, but I'm interrupting you for a reason. Are you all Muslims?" I already knew the answer, but I had to spark a conversation.

They replied, "Yes, we are.

They asked me in turn, "Are you a Christian?"

I replied with a smile, full of His Spirit, "Yes, I am a Christian. But that's not important right now because that word has lost its meaning in America. Maybe not in the underground Church in China or India, where persecution is intense, but in America, everyone's a Christian. So I don't want to confuse you. I'm a follower, lover of God and Jesus. I worship the God of Abraham, Isaac, Jacob, and He loves you, and He's the only one. So don't ask me if I'm a Christian anymore. Ask me if I met God, if I love God. And I will share more clearly what the Bible says a Christian is."

I continued. "Jesus Christ, He spoke to me this morning. So my question to you is not if you are a Muslim or if you go to the mosque. My question to all of you now is, did Allah or Mohammed speak to you this morning? Is Muhammad your friend and is he close by? And if he is, what did he say?"

I briefly shared my testimony with them—of hell, suicide, Heaven, and seeing Jesus. They all listened intently, and then about 8 of the youth seemed confused, some even open and curious. They quickly texted on their phone, and another handful of Muslim youths joined the circle in the gym.

Some replied, "No, he didn't talk to me. I don't even know what it means to be Muslim yet. How did you see hell and Heaven? What did Jesus say to you when you met Him?"

However, there was one student there who was training to become an imam, the equivalent of a pastor in Christianity. He said, "Steve, thanks for sharing, and I want your phone number." I asked him why and he replied, "We want to invite you to our mosque, check out our worship time. Have a debate with our imam. You're talking some sense, but I don't agree with you. Come and have a debate." I gave him my number, and we are praying for the right time for it.

## REACHING OUT

We preach Christ, and Him crucified. We encourage others to do the same, for churches to go outside the four walls and to be on fire daily to save souls. When we encounter those who never met Jesus or have left church, God releases words of knowledge, prophetic words, He heals the sick—and as we share Jesus with the lost, people come to Jesus Christ every week. Those who are poor in spirit, broken, hopeless, lonely, afflicted, and sick of the lies of this world, all receive Jesus, whether big or small, poor or at times rich. Every week we go out to save souls.

With a group of high school and middle school Christian youths, we went to the Irvine Spectrum in Orange County, California, to save souls on a Saturday. The youth pastor in Irvine asked me to equip and evangelize his youth group for the harvest. About 50 students ranging in age from 12 to 18 years old, some with guitars, showed up. I was very glad and encouraged, and even felt the anointing that was on them. After we gathered, we praised God in the middle of Irvine Spectrum, and then we started crying out in prayer, Pentecostal style.

Jesus showed up in the middle of the Irvine Spectrum outdoor shopping mall. It was the year 2024, and many people came aside pointing their smartphones at us. They recorded our outreach and took photos. *Oh how cute,* maybe some of them thought. A handful people joined our circle of young saints in worship.

Then seemingly out of nowhere, a dozen or so security guards approached us. One of the security guards, a young man, came up to me and said, "This is illegal." I replied, "You are illegal." No, I did not say that. I was actually thinking that in my head. To be frank, no church gathers and prays at the Irvine Spectrum as we did, knowing the legal limitations and environment there. The head of security told me, "Nobody does this without permission at the Spectrum, Steve. You need to get a permit next time, get a table on the side, in the corner."

I kept thinking, *Christ is not in the corner. He is the cornerstone, He does not hide in some corner.* I replied to the security officer, "Sorry but this is not illegal, and we are going to preach, regardless, even if it is."

He replied, "You all need to leave. That's it. I'm calling my boss. We're calling the police."

I replied, "Go ahead. They need Jesus too."

Another said, "Are you serious? You want us to call the cops?"

I said, "Yes. Bring them all over. The whole battalion. Bring them here. We want to pray for them too."

The head of security of Irvine Spectrum arrived in no time, and we had a rather civil conversation. He initially said, "I'm a Christian too, Steve. I get your fire. I'm a Mormon myself."

I was filled with joy, until he told me he was Mormon. Mormons do not believe in the Gospel, and it's considered a cult according to biblical and born-again, Jesus-loving Christians.

The head of security told us to go shopping and disperse, otherwise we would be escorted out. Out of our desire to see souls saved that day, we divided the kids into groups of two or three, and sent them out into the mall. When we regathered for debriefing after that evening, we found that all 50 or so young kids talked to someone for the first time to share Jesus, preached the Gospel, handed out tracts, and grew in their boldness to evangelize. God can use anyone, regardless of age or experience, who wants to share the love of Jesus with all people.

## "GO INTO THE MOSQUE"

One day some years ago, I was going to Ralph's, a supermarket chain in California, to buy some food. The Lord spoke to me, "My son, Steve." I was like, uh oh, "Yes, Lord?" His Spirit spoke to me clearly, "Go into the mosque, the Islamic center of Orange County, and tell them I love them." I replied, "Amen." I thought to myself, *Uh oh. I should have not said amen. I'm not going there, Lord. It cannot be You speaking to me for such a task.* He comforted me, "Every temple, church, human being, institution, and nation is Mine. Go inside, and share about Me."

So, I walked into the mosque and looked around. The imam came out to greet me, "How can I help you?"

I replied with a smile, "Sir, I did not want to bother your worship service." I looked behind him, and saw many people praying inside the mosque. I continued, "I was minding my own business and going to buy groceries, but Jesus asked me to come inside here to share that He loves you very much, and all the people here. You guys are bowing to the wrong God. Not Allah, but Jehovah, Jesus is our God, and Muhammad is not the true prophet. Jesus is the Prophet. I know you believe something else, but can I tell you something? Jesus spoke to me this morning. He spoke to me right before I got here. He wants you to know that He died for your sins."

He looked very surprised and perplexed and replied, "My name is Muhammad." Then he signaled to other Muslim brothers in the building and they came over, one by one. I learned that many of the business owners on the street attended this mosque. He asked me to meet him and the others outside of their service. He gave me his phone number and I met him and his mosque members later, outside the building.

From that initial meeting, one of the members invited me to his business, and he brought all of his family and cousins, and even friends to hear what I had to share with them. He introduced me to his family and friends, saying, "Meet Mohammed. Meet my nephew, Mohammed. Meet our security guard, Mohammed. Meet my firstborn Mohammed and second-born Mohammed." I was even invited to their family dinners. Though only one person accepted Christ during these gatherings, a younger brother, I am so grateful that seeds of the Gospel were planted.

Contrary to what the media portrays, many Muslims are hospitable, kind, civil, and very curious about Christianity. However, some of older Muslims did not want to hear anything more about Jesus. "We are Muslims. You can stop telling us about Him," they told me.

Why do I share this story with you, my reader friend? Another time, I preached the Gospel to 300 Muslims in the middle of their service on the lawn of University of California, Irvine. Where does the supernatural boldness come from? I am not crazy. I am a very rational human being who does not like conflict. Yes, I am bold, but I am fearful too at times, to be frank. I share these stories because this is what the Holy Spirit leads, empowers, and then guides us to do—to preach the Gospel to all creation!

Yes, the church in America is bold, but it is at times too fearful to share Jesus with the rest of the world. Where does the calling and the boldness of God come from for us to go out and preach the Gospel? It comes from the Holy Spirit Himself.

Pastor Vlad Savchuk in his book *Host the Holy Ghost* shares what happens to people when the Holy Spirit comes upon them. We no longer need to force ourselves to go out. He Himself pushes us to go out and share Jesus with anyone willing to listen. I do not try to go evangelize or save souls. The Holy Spirit and the love of Christ compels me, us, to do so.

> *For the love of Christ compels us, because we judge thus: that if One died for all, then all died; and He died for all, that those who live should live no longer for themselves, but for Him who died for them and rose again* (2 Corinthians 5:14-15 NKJV).

We do not simply have "evangelism teams." It is more than teams, it is foremost a "lifestyle." Christ Jesus said Himself said that His food is to do the will of the Father in Heaven.

> *Jesus answered them and said, "Most assuredly, I say to you, you seek Me, not because you saw the signs, but because you ate of the loaves and were filled"* (John 6:26 NKJV).

You picked up and are reading this book maybe because you wanted to know more about hell, and how to avoid going there. Maybe you picked it up because you want to save others from going there. Either way, I am so glad God is stirring you up toward His calling in your life.

Jesus taught us to stop laboring for food that perishes. We do not work for money or for temporal earthly pleasure and goals—we live to save souls.

> *Do not labor for the food which perishes, but for the food which endures to everlasting life, which the Son of Man will give you, because God the Father has set His seal on Him* (John 6:27 NKJV).

When my mentor, Pastor Joseph Lee, told me to go find a job, it initially hurt my pride as a pastor. I was a full-time pastor my whole life after meeting Jesus Christ. My mentor was a full-time pastor too, yet he asked me to get a job. He further added, "You're an evangelist. You need to save souls in the workplace. Get out there." My wife was also happier when I sought and secured a job and began to share the Gospel in my sales meetings and with my colleagues. One time, I had an eight-hour conversation with a coworker, by God's grace, and he now attends church.

## AN EVANGELISM LIFESTYLE

Jesus teaches us a spiritual secret. He says to stop laboring for food that spoils and to work for the food that endures to eternal life, which the Son of Man gives us. God the Father has set His seal of full approval on Him already.

> *Do not work for food that spoils, but for food that endures to eternal life, which the Son of Man will give you. For on him God the Father has placed his seal of approval* (John 6:27 NIV).

Evangelism is indeed the work of God. Trust Him. Trust Him 100 percent, 150 percent. Trust Jesus that all your family members are going to come to Christ Jesus this year and be saved.

I urge you to pray, "Father God, save my aunt, save my uncle, save my neighbor, save my boss, save my friends, my children, and my parents. In Jesus' name, in Jesus' name, amen and amen."

As you pray that prayer, angels from Heaven are sent to everyone you prayed for, even now.

My uncle came to Christ Jesus, after 15 years of praying for him. He was a gangster in South Korea. He used to carry a hammer around and got into many fights and dangers. Now he is a born-again Christian who reads his Bible daily and trusts in Jesus. We prayed for him for 15 years. My father also, after 10 years of prayer, met Jesus Christ personally and powerfully. He is now on fire for Jesus Christ. He is an evangelist himself and many call him a saint in the church he attends, Grace Church. Praise Jesus! He and my mother are my number-one intercessors and support for my ministry, along with my wife.

## PRAY ALWAYS

Why do we pray for souls to be saved? We pray because many are thirsty and hungry for life, deliverance, salvation, and help from the God of love and holiness, Jesus Christ!

> *And He said to me, "It is done! I am the Alpha and the Omega, the Beginning and the End. I will give of the fountain of the water of life freely to him who thirsts. He who overcomes shall inherit all things, and I will be his God and he shall be My son. But the cowardly, unbelieving, abominable, murderers, sexually immoral, sorcerers, idolaters, and all liars shall have their part in the lake which burns with fire and brimstone, which is the second death"* (Revelation 21:6-8 NKJV).

We pray to become overcomers. We pray to stay away from cowardice, unbelief, idolatry, hatred or murder, immorality, sorcery, and lying. We pray because prayer helps us to stay strong and in Jesus Christ! We also pray because Jesus answers prayers. When we pray, His will is done on earth, as it is in Heaven!

> *This is the will of the Father who sent Me, that of all He has given Me I should lose nothing, but should raise it up at the last day. And this is the will of Him who sent Me, that everyone who sees the Son and believes in Him may have everlasting life; and I will raise him up at the last day* (John 6:39-40 NKJV).

I was with my friends one night at dinner. They shared with me, "I heard Jesus Center is a good church."

I replied, "It is, we are all about saving souls."

They replied, "Take us with you."

"Come with me. Let's go," I replied and added, "Shut your church down if it is not saving souls."

Sorry, but I am a little blunt when it comes to issues of eternal consequences. I am a bit straightforward when we talk about Heaven and hell, and evangelism. Jesus did not pull back or sugarcoat the truth when it came to saving souls. God is not asking us to be politically correct this season. We cannot win souls by being politically correct or by being nice people. Kindness is a fruit of the Spirit. However, only the message of repentance and the Cross will lead people out of misery, bondage, and hell. Only those who pray by faith and obey will be used by God to share the truth of His Gospel!

God is cleaning His house right now during this season. Many false prophets, fake pastors, sinful leaders are being exposed. This is why the apostle Paul says, *"But I discipline my body and bring it into subjection, lest, when I have preached to others, I myself should become disqualified"* (1 Corinthians 9:27 NKJV).

It is not only about how we look or act when with are with others, but what we do afterward. I try to keep busy studying, reading, praying, and staying focused on the Lord and His work when alone. I am grateful for my wife who has sanctified me through marriage; and as Rabbi Daniel Lapin teaches, it is an honor to provide for and fight for my wife.

We store up treasures in Heaven by loving the unlovable, blessing the unblessable, forgiving the unforgivable, serving those who cannot repay us, and we stop worrying about our reputation.

Let us pray once more:

*Lord Jesus, I want Your heart for souls. I want to be empowered by Your Spirit, to be Your witness. Let us see people come to You wherever we go. We thank You for the vision You gave us for thousands of souls to come into Your Kingdom this year. Through each of us, people will be led back to God. We thank You, God, for the harvest that is coming upon the face of the earth, despite all the darkness and destruction that looms, encourage us and send us to the harvest field.*

*Give us the urgency of Heaven, Father God. We thank You, God. We decree, prophesy, declare, and proclaim by faith, in agreement with our Lord and Savior, Your Son Jesus Christ, that this is the year of the evangelist. So let miracles break forth, God. Let prophetic words open up hearts to You, and to Your love and to Your healing.*

*Let us see inner healing and deliverance on the streets and everywhere we go, even within our churches. Let us be merciful as You are merciful. We want to have great rewards that last, from You, Father God! In Your mercy, save souls! In Jesus' name we pray, amen.*

Here is what the lifestyle and heart of the truly born-again Christian looks like, those who do not go to hell—those have a sure road to Heaven! Jesus teaches it very plainly and clearly:

*But to you who are listening I say: Love your enemies, do good to those who hate you, bless those who curse you, pray for those who mistreat you. If someone slaps you on one cheek, turn to them the other also. If someone takes your coat, do not withhold your shirt from them. Give to everyone who asks you, and if anyone takes what belongs to you, do not demand it back. Do to others as you would have them do to you.*

*If you love those who love you, what credit is that to you? Even sinners love those who love them. And if you do good to those who are good to you, what credit is that to you? Even sinners do that. And if you lend to those from whom you expect repayment, what credit is that to you? Even sinners lend to sinners, expecting to be repaid in full. But love your enemies, do good to them, and lend to them without expecting to get anything back. Then* ***your reward will be great, and you will be children of the Most High****, because he is kind to the ungrateful and wicked. Be merciful, just as your Father is merciful* (Luke 6:27-36 NIV).

# 15

# THE MOST BEAUTIFUL ACT OF LOVE

We ask ourselves this question: "What can I do for the ones I love?" Some of what we can do include serving, sharing, giving, and praying for them. However, if they do not know Jesus, the most precious and valuable thing we can do for them is to share the reality of Heaven and hell with them.

Also share with them the fact that Jesus is God's beloved Son and that they can be God's children by faith. As His children, we can communicate with God, and we can share with others that anyone can go to Heaven through faith in Jesus, by having a personal and intimate relationship with Him. All are welcome, if they repent and surrender to Him as not just Savior, but also as Lord and King. I truly believe that this is the most beautiful act of love one can show for the people close to them and for every soul we meet.

Your work, your labor, your business activities can be the place to complete the missional work for the world. Where you stand, your workplace, can be where you complete your heavenly mission. You can be the way for the Holy Spirit and you can be the worshiper, the steward, and the good influential leader to complete God's world mission! What a great heavenly call! Workplace Mission. This is the heavenly calling itself.

Mission fills the gap between Heaven and earth and firmly connects the two. Mission is heavenly culture and completely different from earthly culture. Entering into mission heavenly culture causes birth to holiness and new life in earthly culture. We believe that this mission task given to God's people who carry out His mission with absolute obedience has been given to workplace ministers who are committed to establishing God's Kingdom on earth through activities in business and workplaces.

We need to understand that our workplaces are also mission fields. The ground where we believers stand is holy ground and a mission field. This mission field is brand-new to many people, especially pastors who were in full-time ministry. Remember, only when the Holy Spirit leads us personally, can we take on this mission task.

Let's review Revelation again and look at what God says about the last day of the world!

> *Then I saw a great white throne and him who was seated on it. From his presence earth and sky fled away, and no place was found for them. And I saw the dead, great and small, standing before the throne, and books were opened. Then another book was opened, which is the book of life. And the dead were judged by what was written in the books, according to what they had done. And the sea gave up the dead who were in it, Death and Hades gave up the dead who were in them, and they were judged, each one of them, according to what they had done. Then Death and Hades were thrown into the lake of fire. This is the second death, the lake of fire. And if anyone's name was not found written in the book of life, he was thrown into the lake of fire.* (Revelation 20:11-15 ESV).

That's right! This world will come to an end with the conclusion God has made. It will be no more and no less. It is as written in the Word. Not one single life can avoid the judgment.

Today, as we deal with the apocalypse and business, we learn and receive from the Scriptures the reason why we must be accurately aware of the end of the world through the words in the books of Revelation and Ezekiel. We need to know exactly why God saved us and why God calls us into the field of business!

We live in this world but we do not follow the ways of this world. We die to the sins of this world and we resurrect for the righteousness of Heaven. We do not live to earn eternal life, rather we live in this world for eternity. We are the ones who inherit eternity in this world that will someday disappear. We stand in this place, the holy place, listening to God's voice as the worshiper, as the steward who brings all the resources God has given to us in this land and to this place. We are to bring as many souls to Christ as possible through good influence and standing firmly between gaps of cultures where we live as we walk with the Holy Spirit.

Lastly, remember the proclamation of Heaven for us in Revelation 21:1-7 (NIV):

> *Then I saw "a new heaven and a new earth," for the first heaven and the first earth had passed away, and there was no longer any sea. I saw the Holy City, the new Jerusalem, coming down out of heaven from God, prepared as a bride beautifully dressed for her husband. And I heard a loud voice from the throne saying, "Look! God's dwelling place is now among the people, and he will dwell with them. They will be his people, and God himself will be with them and be their God. 'He will wipe every tear from their eyes. There will be no more death' or mourning or crying or pain, for the old order of things has passed away."*
>
> *He who was seated on the throne said, "I am making everything new!" Then he said, "Write this down, for these words are trustworthy and true."*
>
> *He said to me: "It is done. I am the Alpha and the Omega, the Beginning and the End. To the thirsty I will give water without cost from the spring of the water of life. Those who are victorious*

> *will inherit all this, and I will be their God and they will be my children."*

The one who conquers will have the inheritance. What rewards do you desire to receive from God when you return home to heaven?

# APPENDIX

# INTERVIEWS DISCUSSING MY NEAR-DEATH EXPERIENCE, HELL, HEAVEN, JESUS CHRIST

To watch the documentary and other videos, please visit the following internet links.

- Angel Studios Platform: https://www.angel.com/livestreams/9b52d76a-dd53-4f3f-af94-f8b4f1348eab
- Steve Kang: From hell to heaven! Ex Buddhist Steve Kang's Testimony of Salvation thru Jesus Christ! GoodtvUSA – https://www.youtube.com/watch?v=a_tjn_FON1w&t=2s
- Precious Testimonies: I CUT MY THROAT AND BELLY OPEN BECAUSE SATAN SAID I WOULD GO TO HEAVEN IF I DID! https://www.youtube.com/watch?v=gk50V-upC_Q&t=1s
- Randy Kay: Near Death Experience: Buddhist Overdoses and Finds Jesus in Heaven – Ep. 26 https://www.youtube.com/watch?v=7ht7nFXey-A&rco=1
- TODAY: SAVED BY GRACE Buddhism to hell to Jesus to Heaven! | TODAY: SAVED BY GRACE
- Pegi Robinson: NDE TV – NDE TV Presents Steve, a Buddhist pre-law student on drugs who stabbed himself and went to hell!
- Isaiah Saldivar Channel: Man CUTS his throat and goes to HELL – This is what he saw!
- https://www.allnationsjc.org/pastor-steve-kang

# ABOUT THE AUTHOR

After almost losing his life in a drug overdose when 19 years old, the Lord Jesus Christ showed Steve Kang Heaven and hell and he became a born-again Christian. He has been serving the Lord through the ups and downs and the thick and thin of ministry and life.

Steve graduated from University of California, Irvine with a Bachelor of Science degree in Economics and earned a Master of Divinity degree from Talbot School of Theology in La Mirada, California. He is the founder of Revive The Nations, a church planting and radical evangelism movement in these last days.

Steve also preaches and serves as an revivalist preacher and church planter in the body of Christ through the SBC Send Network. Steve Kang also served on the mission field in China and as a Chaplain 1st Lieutenant in the US Army. Steve works as a consultant to Kingdom business owners.

Steve is married to Goeun Kim, a loving wife and professional pianist for church worship. They live in Orange County, California.

# CONTACT INFORMATION

www.allnationsjc.org
www.schoolofministers.com